D0342738

Home Guide to
Lawns and
Landscaping

A Popular Science Book

Home Guide to
Lawns and Landscaping

by Bruce Cassiday

Drawings by
Frank Schwarz

POPULAR SCIENCE

HARPER & ROW

New York, Evanston, San Francisco, London

Copyright © 1976 by Bruce Cassiday
Published by Book Division, Times Mirror Magazines, Inc.

Brief quotations may be used in critical articles and reviews.
For any other reproduction of the book, however, including elec-
tronic, mechanical, photocopying, recording or other means, writ-
ten permission must be obtained from the publisher

Library of Congress Catalog Card Number: 75-40601
ISBN: 0-06-010689-1

Eighth Printing, 1978

Manufactured in the United States of America

Contents

ACKNOWLEDGMENTS

A great many people contributed to the preparation of this book. I'd like to thank especially Donald Ferlow, Gilbert B. Wheless, Jr., and Dennis Laferriere of Environmental Design Associates of Stamford, Conn.; Dr. Edward Duda, of the University of Connecticut at Bartlett Aboretum, Stamford, Conn.; and August Lenniger, Hal Steeger, and Forest Belt, who all helped with photographs and/or identification of plants. For their various appreciated services, I'd also like to thank the California Redwood Association, Frank Burgmeier and the Jacobsen Manufacturing Company, Sam Nuspliger of the Society of the Plastics Industry, and the Toro Company and the Disston Company. Cathy Cassiday helped with photographs of landscapes and specimens, and Doris Cassiday helped with identification of plants.

SPECIAL NOTE ON CHEMICAL GARDEN CONTROLS

The formulations for chemical controls of weeds, pests, and fungus growths in this book were all recommended at the time the manuscript was prepared. Chemical controls are constantly being discarded, adopted, or perfected by manufacturers. New chemicals are tested by the Environmental Protection Agency in Washington. If proved effective according to the manufacturer's claims, the formulation is granted an EPA registration number, which is stamped on every container. The home gardener can be assured that if he uses an EPA registered chemical for a particular weed, pest, or fungus listed on the container, and follows the directions scrupulously, he will not be endangering his garden, his pets, or the environment. The gardener who needs a specific chemical control for a particular weed, pest, or fungus should contact his local Department of Agriculture county agent.

Home Guide to
Lawns and
Landscaping

1 Landscape Planning

BARE LAND IS AN AFFRONT to nature. If land is cleared, plant life of all shapes, sizes, and forms immediately takes root and grows. Of all the plants that try to grow, only the hardiest survive. Unless the soil is infertile or the climate outside the range of life, any strip of cleared land will soon be covered with foliage.

A wild landscape will be filled by wild plants. Not all such plants are particularly attractive or desirable. Control must be exerted over the growth on any section of earth. If the plot is the site of a home all growing things come under the management of the homeowner. He is in charge of the landscaping: the planning, selection, and maintenance of the proper plants on the residential property.

Within the past ten years there has been an unrestricted flow of humanity from the crowded cities of America to the less crowded sections outside the city, that part of the environment called suburbia. Suburban lots generally range in size from a quarter-acre to a half-acre. With plots that small, and with techniques and technological improvements making effective gardening possible for everyone, the art of landscaping a suburban lot has become one of the most important and interesting features of modern living.

THE PART FOLIAGE PLAYS. Although the house itself is the focal point of any suburban lot, the appearance of the foliage around it is also important. Foliage makes a house seem right in its location and provides the background to help make the total picture attractive. The background includes all forms of plant life – the lawn, big plants and little ones.

If you consider the homesite a picture, the lawn is the horizontal base, the trees the vertical altitude, and the flowering shrubs the spots of color that bring the picture to life.

As with painting, a total artistic effect can be achieved through many different ways. The homeowner can plan a symmetrically balanced landscape, an asymmetrical one, or a dramatic combination of the two. But no matter what kind of relationship exists between house and foliage, the structure itself must fit snugly into its environment. It should seem as permanent an object on the land as all the growth about it. A house that has been well-landscaped will have a permanence and an inevitability to it. A badly landscaped house will look as if it had been dropped down on a bare strip of ground without any thought or preparation.

HOW TO SOFTEN STRUCTURAL LINES. A house tends to be angular and composed of straight lines set at right angles to one another. But such stiff geometric precision defeats the naturalness the homeowner is striving to achieve and makes the house seem alien to its environment.

Three important types of plantings are used to break up the dreadful formality of man-made horizontals and verticals: lawns, trees, and shrubs.

All of these plantings grow in soft, informal lines – circles, curves, arcs, and combinations of these – and tend to neutralize the harshness of machine-made construction. They help the building to blend with the ground on which it sits.

1

Three primary types of planting — tree, shrub, and lawn — act not only as harmonizing factors to soften harsh construction lines, but lead the eye directly to the entrance. Egg-shaped hemlock and pillbox-shaped yew, edged by pachysandra, are bordered with andromeda and mountain laurel.

Flowering dogwood is in perfect scale with portion of house it borders. Note how foundation planting of azalea and ground cover of pachysandra are in scale both with the house and tree. Towering pines make a perfect natural backdrop for setting.

Keep in mind, too, that technological improvements—heat, insulation, and increased use of "picture-window" glass—have made outdoor living possible even for people dwelling in the cooler parts of the country. When you plan your landscape, think of trees and sky as part of your living quarters; include garden, lawn, and plants in the over-all design of your house's interior.

THE ART OF LANDSCAPING. In order to achieve the proper harmony between house and land, you can use the methods of professional landscapers. The professional studies the house and existing foliage, making note of whatever attractive design elements can be enhanced. Then, he chooses new plant materials which will emphasize the strong points in the original design and compensate for its lacks.

In making his analysis, the professional landscaper bears in mind the following elements borrowed from the visual arts field: unity, scale, balance, proportion, shape, color, texture, rhythm and focal point. You, too, can successfully plan your own landscape if you analyze your property in terms of each of these elements.

Unity. To provide unity, all plantings in a single site must be related by form, by color, and/or texture. When too many disparate objects are thrown into juxtaposition with one another, the eye cannot settle on any one point, and keeps restlessly moving from one to the other, without enjoying any.

Scale. The size of any plant is an important consideration. A large tree may be used to frame a house, to give shade to a terrace, or to screen out some objectionable sight. A small tree may be used to carry out the low, flat design of a ranch house, to make it seem longer and flatter.

The plant must be *in scale* with the house and with the rest of the plantings. Too large a tree can crush a small house. Too small a tree can make a large, ungainly house seem even larger.

Balance. Stability in artistic composition depends on correct balance, whether it be symmetrical or asymmetrical. The same is true of landscape composition.

Plants grown evenly around some central element—a plot of bright flowers, a rock garden with showy cactus spikes, or a reflecting pool—will give the scene symmetrical balance.

A large window or an entranceway that is at one side of a house can be balanced by a large tree at one side and a small one at the opposite, or by a clump of birches at one side and a single tree at the opposite. This type of balance is asymmetrical.

Proportion. Proportion in composition is the relationship of one part to another, and of each to the whole. It is linked to the concepts of scale and balance.

As you choose any plant for your landscape you must think of its size at maturity and how it will relate to the rest of the site.

Two mistakes of proportion made by many amateurs can be seen on suburban sites:

(1) Border shrubs grow too big and tend to crowd each other out. At maturity, they are not in proportion with the path, walk, or driveway they border.

(2) Many evergreen shrubs grow too big and dominate a house; they may even bury it under a heavy texture of green. They are not in proportion with the house and lot.

Both these mistakes can be avoided by remembering one cardinal rule of thumb:

Most plants grow faster and require more room than you think when you plant them.

Golden varieties of evergreen specimens are valued for the permanence of their color tones. At left, golden arborvitae produces almost frosty outer texture, with golden plumed cypress, center, and golden thread cypress, right, presenting yellowish rather than green hues for special planting.

Rhythm is achieved by use of repetition, as with these birches planted against fairly regular lines of steps.

A broad-leaved evergreen, the boxwood, serves as foundation plants against this house, providing year-round landscaping.

Shape. The *shape* of any plant is as important as its size. It may be globular like a lollipop, or it may be domed like a derby. Trees like the fir, the hemlock, or the holly may have a pyramidal shape. And the weeping willow appears to droop. All manner of plant shapes are available for whatever effect you may wish to create.

Color. Another aspect of any plant is the potential color of its foliage or blossoms. Even without blossoming, some trees appear to be all of one color; others seem to be of two or more shades of green because of the spacing of their leaves and branches. Evergreen trees hold one solid color throughout the year; deciduous trees turn yellow, orange, or red in the autumn.

Flowering plants — trees, shrubs, and flowers — can be dramatically effective in adding spots of color to the over-all landscape composition. Choose them wisely and place them judiciously.

Texture. The textural surface of any object is an important consideration in art and in landscaping. Each plant has its own particular texture depending on the size of the leaves, on the way they are attached to the stems, and on the way they are spaced on the branch.

Each plant appears as either rough or smooth, dull or shiny, or thick or thin. Texture creates mood and gives a sense of movement and light to a landscape.

Rhythm. The trickiest part of artistic design is rhythm, the recurrence of certain accents of color or shape. In landscape planting, you can gain a feeling of movement by repeating the same plant, or group of plants, in different parts of the site. A low dwarf Mugho pine repeated in edgings, in foundation plantings, and in individual specimens throughout the yard will give the observer a sense of movement and excitement. The recurrence of a bright-colored flower at intervals in a garden will draw the observer's eye along swiftly in anticipation of its next appearance.

You can vary repetition slightly by choosing different varieties of the same general species, and by planting them singly in one area, doubly in another, and triply in a third.

Focal point. When properly applied, all the preceding tricks of landscaping design will lead the eye to the focal point of a design. This may be some unusual and even expensive specimen which carries the weight of the entire picture: a weeping birch; a Japanese cherry tree; a flowering dogwood; a rugged old apple tree. The focal point of your homesite is the reason for all the surrounding detail. You can use the full extent of your ingenuity in choosing it.

These, then, are the basic elements of landscape design. Let's see how you can apply them to your house and lot.

THE THREE LIVING AREAS. In planning the landscaping around a house, you must attack the problem from a practical angle as well as from an esthetic one. A plant will add a great deal to the visual attractiveness of any home; a plant can, on the other hand, be a ghastly eyesore if it is improperly placed so as to interfere with any practical living situation.

For this reason, it is important to divide the homesite into the three areas that are involved in day-to-day living: the public area, the private area, and the service area.

The public area. The area in front of the house and on both sides — sometimes in the rear — is called the "public area," and it includes all that is in view from outside the property. This area includes part of the house, a great deal of the lawn, some shrubs, border plants, edgings, and hedges that are in front of or to the side of the house. Here is the place where your imagination and artistic perceptions can really come into play. All plantings here must set off the house in dramatic fashion.

A low, flat house (a ranch) can be made to look even wider and more sprawling by the judicious use of certain foundation plants and by putting low, flat shrubs at each end.

A high, two-story house (an old-fashioned salt box) can be set off by tall, slender trees looming up on each side of it, and by foundation plants that form vertical lines.

A formal Georgian house — of brick, with large rectangular windows and shutters — can be enhanced by carefully shaped hedges and clipped shrubs at windows and doorway.

A Cape Cod house — not too high and not too wide — can be complemented by the judicious use of evergreen shrubs that are both round and square-trimmed.

In planning the public area of your house, you will decide on shapes that will bring house and landscape together in as pleasing a way as possible. The main point to remember in planning any landscape planting is to make use of the contour of the earth and the lines of the house simultaneously.

The private area. This second area of the homesite includes all of the inside of the house and all the yard that is invisible from the front, except for the third area, which is called the "service area." The private area is that part of your home in which you do most of your living, and in which you want seclusion.

The backyard of most properties is part of the private area, and so is part of each side of the house. It is in these sections that a great many different plantings can be effectively displayed.

The most used part of the backyard is the recreational section, where the children play and the family entertains outdoors. This section includes the barbecue pit, the terrace or patio, and any stretch of grass used for sunbathing and/or entertaining.

It is in the private area that special mini-gardens are located, like the flower garden, usually protected by plantings; a vegetable garden; fruit trees and vines; a rock garden; a goldfish pond; a bonsai section.

As the swimming pool becomes more commonplace in suburban America, it

Foundation plants of azalea and yew and ground cover of pachysandra mask the flat foundation of this formal house, and dogwoods soften angularity of the design.

Yew and arborvitae shrubs can be used as picturesque border to screen an ugly service area containing garbage cans. Note how ground ivy is used to conceal gaps at the base of the shrubs.

frequently becomes the focal point of a family's entire private area, with plantings that beautify the pool environment.

Because these various sections of the private area are used for such different pursuits, each of them should be separated from the other. Hedges, edgings, and plantings of shrubs and trees can be used for this purpose.

It is of primary importance that you locate each section of the private area in its proper place so that the whole will be in harmony with the public and service areas and will not interfere with the practical matters of day-to-day living.

The service area. The third area of the suburban house is called the "service area," and is that part of the homesite reserved for garbage collection, entrance and exit for servicemen, and tool sheds, workshops, and woodboxes.

This area should be screened from the rest of the homesite. A fence or thick hedge can keep the garbage collection site invisible in the backyard, or the service area may be placed in a position where it cannot be seen from front or back. An individual tree can often conceal it, or a bushy, thick shrub.

Toolsheds, greenhouses, or storage sheds can be screened in the same way. They can be covered by climbing vines, or concealed by shrubs, hedges, or trees.

Ingenious homeowners have even placed sheds and woodboxes in the middle of the yard behind stones used to form rock gardens. Others have placed utility sheds behind screens of bright flowers, or even behind annuals hung in flower boxes on redwood screening walls.

There are many different ways you can screen out these undesirable sights. Natural landscaping is the best way; wooden or metal structures are obtrusive and unnatural.

PLANNING YOUR LANDSCAPE. The procedure for planning the landscape around your house is to start with what you have and then add plantings to enhance both structure and terrain and blend them together in as harmonious a package as possible.

The first step is to draw a simple bird's-eye view of your lot and house, and sketch in everything—trees, shrubs, slopes, rocks, grass.

In order to get the proportions right—the actual scale of the house in relation to the lot—draw the plan on graph paper and let one square represent a square foot.

To do this, measure the outside of the house and draw it in scale. Draw the driveway and any walks, along with all trees or shrubs that are presently growing. Mark in all utility lines—telephone wires and power wires. It is usually a good idea to show the location of septic tank, cesspool, or sewer lines in case any of them has to be dug up for any reason. Be sure not to plan a tree or shrub too near a sewer line, and never plan a tree or shrub over a septic tank. Draw in large rocks that cannot be moved and indicate slopes by showing ascent and descent with arrows.

By the time you have finished the preliminary sketch, you should have a good idea where to begin with your planning.

The second step is to determine what you would like to have on your lot in addition to what you already have. Start first with practical considerations, including things you need that you do not have. For instance (see opposite):

(1) The house next door is ugly; you want a screen to keep it out of sight.

(2) The sun hits your house full force in the late afternoon; you want some shade.

(3) The wind blows up the hillside in the back and keeps the ground too cold in the winter; you want a windscreen in back.

(4) A steep slope in the backyard erodes during spring thaw; you want plantings to keep the soil in place.

WIND 3

BAD SLOPE 4

UGLY HOUSE 1

2

STREET TOO CLOSE

AFTERNOON SUN

5

Illustration shows how to translate landscaping needs into plantings. The problem is analyzed in detail in the accompanying text.

(5) The front of the house is high, wide, and overpowering on approach; you want plantings to take the frontage back from the street.

Draw in these five needs by translating them to landscape features, as shown in the drawing above.

(1) Add a hedge as screen, or a row of evergreen trees.

(2) Add a shade tree to protect the side of the house that gets too much afternoon sunshine.

(3) Add a windscreen of chokecherry or Chinese elm across the back.

(4) Add a groundcover of pachysandra or creeping myrtle for the steep slope to prevent erosion.

(5) Add small foundation plants like evergreens, textured ground cover, and possibly a specimen tree to take the eye away from the house front.

Simple classic design of small yard needs careful trimming to keep the ground cover and flower bed in circular shape and the pathway clear.

CHOOSING A STYLE. The third step in your planning is choosing among four basic landscape design styles.

(1) Formal design. Balance is symmetrical.

(2) Informal design. Balance is achieved leisurely and without complete symmetry.

(3) Combination formal-informal design. Formal and informal design are blended.

(4) Natural design. Nature is blended carefully with the house.

Actually, the differences among the four types of design are sometimes quite difficult to distinguish. Parts of each can be interchanged with parts of others. Conventional design uses squares and circles and triangles and balance; natural design uses nature's own circles and straight edges for harmonious combinations.

Formal design. This style makes use of rigid circles, arcs, squares, rectangles, and formally executed pathways, drives, and sidewalks. Formal design is strictly balanced design. You can divide the garden in the middle, placing no more foliage on one side of the center than on the other.

You can obtain an extremely pleasing effect by formal planting of this type. You must keep all lawns, shrubs, and trees trimmed, all paths and drives neatly edged. You can use retaining walls and pathways to keep rigid, unwavering lines. Clear definition of shapes and edges is essential in a formal garden.

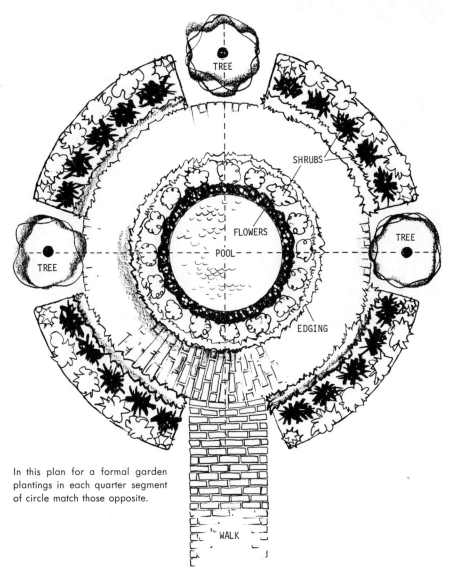

TREE

SHRUBS

FLOWERS

POOL

TREE

TREE

EDGING

In this plan for a formal garden
plantings in each quarter segment
of circle match those opposite.

WALK

You can avoid monotony by making the lawn on several different levels, or by constructing terraces to change the earth's contour.

The formal garden comes to us from Europe and from the classical past when patterns were strict and undeviating.

Informal design. Here certain deviations from formal balance are permitted. The informal garden comes to us from Japan. You can let the lawn slope a bit from one side of the lot to the other. You can plant groups of one kind of shrub on the left, and nothing but flowers on the right. You can use rocks to balance heavy trees opposite them. You can let shrubs remain unclipped. You can let trees follow the earth's natu-

California Redwood Assoc.

Informal outdoor garden shows how various types of plantings can be mixed, along with stones and rock slabs.

ral line. Pathways can curve and meander. You can use mini-gardens of rock, pool lilies, hanging baskets, and almost anything imaginable. You can even add natural rock, crushed stone for mulch, crushed marble for pathways, and other natural objects for effect.

Formal-informal design. A combination formal-informal design can give your grounds a pleasing look. You can start out with straight lines, careful curves, and formal setting of clipped hedges, clipped trees, and strictly mowed lawns, and combine them with portions of unclipped hedges, rough-textured ground cover, and untrimmed plants that act as counterpoint to the formal lines.

Today's style of living — with its emphasis on outdoor activities — tends to the informal. Yet there is comfort in using traditional concepts along with the informal. You can have a trimly clipped box hedge running as background to a group of unclipped, wild mountain laurels growing in a mulch of crushed rock. Or you can combine a formally mowed lawn with an area of no-maintenance groundcover like myrtle or pachysandra.

Natural design. Interest in ecology and the relation of man to his environment has inspired a new concept in gardening: the natural look. This style has also been encouraged by the suburban gardener's desire to reduce his working time. The "natural look" can be said to be the lazy man's excuse for demanding an essentially "no-maintenance" landscape.

The natural look in landscaping emphasizes the blending of the house with its natural environment — rocks where they exist, sand or gravel where it lies, the growth of

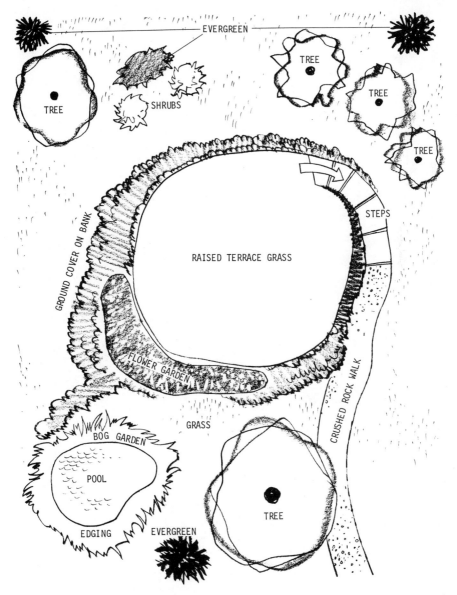

In this informal garden plan, both sides of imaginary center line are in balance. The raised terrace provides elevation that serves as a focal point for the entire garden.

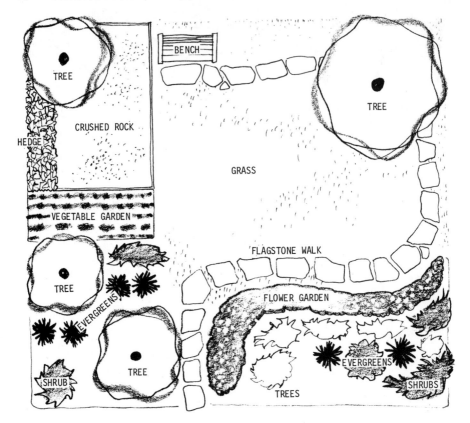

Mixture of formal and informal garden planning should display a certain symmetrical balance. The rectangular area at upper left offsets the looser area of shrubs at lower right.

plants indigenous to the region. Natural landscaping also avoids the use of lawn grass where it is extremely difficult to grow. And this, of course, cuts down on maintenance for you.

Instead of setting a dwelling down in the midst of a hostile environment and trying to shape the environment to conform rigidly to it, you do exactly the opposite: you landscape the area around the house to bring it into closer harmony with nature.

Texture is a primary consideration in the natural look. The rough ground cover blends with the rough foundation plantings; these in turn blend with the rough texture of the trees and foliage surrounding the house. An accent in slick, feathery, or shimmering foliage will then play against the rough texture in a complementary fashion.

You use bank plantings to accentuate the natural landscape: juniper and cotoneaster to give color and texture. You build steps of crushed rock blocked out with railroad ties or timbers, with begonias planted alongside and sedum growing in between rocks alongside the steps.

You tailor the earth to your needs without making the tailoring look artificial. You landscape a terrace or a patio with natural stone, slate, flagstone, or other living rock. Or you build a terrace and plant it with hard grass to withstand walking and sitting.

You give your yard elevations by a judicious moving of earth, rather than smoothing over all the rough spots for a bowling-green – and artificial – smoothness.

Along with conventional plantings – formal, informal, and formal-informal – you'll find many examples of the natural look in the pages of this book. Try it if you like it – it's the coming thing in landscape design in this ecological age.

SKETCHING YOUR GROUNDS. The fourth step in planning your landscaping is to sit back and imagine how you want the scene around your house to look. Think of background and foundation plants, and lawn, and walk, and driveway – everything. In this phase of planning you can let your imagination run wild. Consider whatever is esthetically pleasing to you.

The plan should begin to take shape. Draw in the shadowy forms, using tree outlines that will carry out the scheme you have in mind. Draw these backgrounds behind the house and to the side of it. And add in anything else you think you might want. Now look at it and measure the actual heights and widths of the trees and shrubs you have imagined. You can figure the sizes by reference to the house itself.

With the shapes converted to measurements, you can look at the chapter on trees and shrubs later in this book in order to locate plants that will fit the heights, sizes, and shapes you want.

Pay particular attention to the size at maturity of any shrub or tree you wish to purchase. In a suburban lot, the most common mistake the amateur gardener can make is to overplant with too many items and/or to overplant with oversized speci-

Use of rough-textured pachysandra ground cover enhances area around the dogwood tree. Note the mixture of evergreens in leucothoë against the wall and the weeping hemlock near the rock which provide an interesting texture.

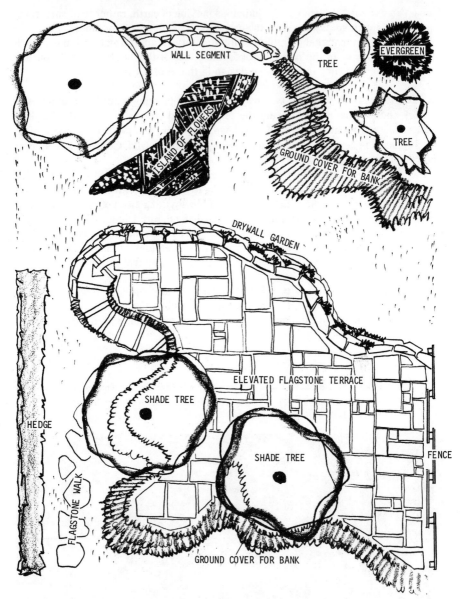

WALL SEGMENT

TREE

EVERGREEN

TREE

ISLAND OF FLOWERS

GROUND COVER FOR BANK

DRYWALL GARDEN

ELEVATED FLAGSTONE TERRACE

SHADE TREE

HEDGE

FLAGSTONE WALK

SHADE TREE

FENCE

GROUND COVER FOR BANK

This drawing shows the balance and flow of a naturally landscaped yard. Banks and elevations are left as they were originally, with only superficial shaping.

PLANT SHAPES FOR LANDSCAPING

mens. Because many lots are bare to begin with, it is a temptation for the panicky homeowner to try to fill all vacancies with instant foliage.

In choosing specific trees, you may not always be able to procure exactly what you want. For example, in Vermont you will not be able to purchase unlimited supplies of eucalyptus trees; they do not grow well in New England and they are not in large supply there. If you are in California, you could buy an unlimited supply of eucalyptus trees. On the other hand, you might not be able to purchase a sugar maple in California as easily as you can in Vermont.

Even if you do not know exactly what kind of trees and/or shrubs are available at your local nursery, you can make out an order list anyway. First list trees, then shrubs, vines, ground covers, and finally flowers. You can estimate the cost by looking at a nursery catalogue. Then make out an order list, including the number of plants, the common name of each, botanical name, height and/or spread, and habit of growth. In this way you can procure almost any kind of tree or shrub you want: high-branched, low-branched, double-trunked, thick, thin, or perhaps a matched pair of trees.

Here is an example of a nursery list for plantings:

NO.	NAME	BOTANICAL NAME	SIZE
		TREES	
1	Flowering dogwood	*Cornus florida*	10' low-branched
1	Japanese pagodatree	*Sophora japonica*	20' wide habit
3	White birch	*Betula pendula alba*	25' high-branched
		SHRUBS	
3	Dwarf andromeda	*Pieris floribunda*	12"
5	White azalea	*Rhododendron indicum 'Niobe'*	18"
3	Swamp azalea	*Rhododendron viscosum*	18"
3	Leucothoe	*Leucothoe fontanesiana*	2'
		GROUND COVER	
	Creeping myrtle	*Vinca minor*	
		FLOWERS	
	Chrysanthemum	*Chrysanthemum morifolium*	yellow
	Marigold	*Tagetes patula*	yellow
	Mixed annuals		

TIPS ON LANDSCAPE PLANNING. In planning any kind of landscape arrangement, you should pay attention to the following rules:

(1) Use varieties of plants that will thrive in your particular geographical and climatic region.

(2) Observe each plant's particular requirements: its liking or disliking of shade; its preference for acid or alkaline soil; its growth qualities; its life expectancy.

(3) Make your planting seem natural: informal spacing for an informal garden; formal positioning for a formal garden; natural placement for a natural garden.

(4) Keep the center of any yard area open so that the eye will be drawn to the distant border: the effect will be one of space and harmony.

(5) Avoid crowding shrubs, flowers, and trees together, or the entire effect will be one of clutter and confusion.

(6) Arrange plants in masses: flowers of all different colors and shapes together; shrubs in groups; trees in pairs. Each enhances the other.

(7) Do not hide dwarf objects behind tall plants, or there will be no point in using dwarfs at all. They should always appear in front to lead the eye to the taller specimens in the rear.

(8) Display good taste in all your arrangements, avoiding astonishing or too-startling effects. All shock does is weary the eye of the beholder.

(9) Purchase plants only from reliable sources so that you can count on proper performance from each plant—or get your money back.

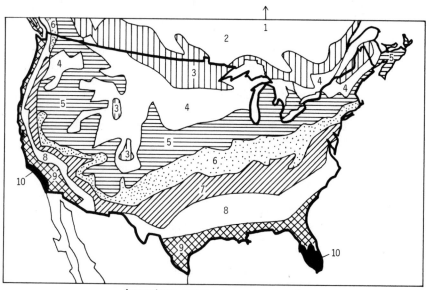

Approximate range of average annual
minimum temperatures for each zone

Zone 1	Below −30	Zone 6	−10 to 0
Zone 2	−50 to −40	Zone 7	0 to 10
Zone 3	−40 to −30	Zone 8	10 to 20
Zone 4	−30 to −20	Zone 9	20 to 30
Zone 5	−20 to −10	Zone 10	30 to 40

The United States has so many different soil and climatic conditions that a plant which grows in Hawaii may not grow in Maine, and vice versa. Horticulturists in conjunction with the United States Department of Agriculture have devised a "hardiness" map of 10 zones to show the northern limits of successful growth for any plant. Generally speaking, the hardiest plants have the lowest numbers. Many nurseries follow the Department of Agriculture's zone numbers in showing where plants will and will not grow. The purchaser should check his geographical zone number and be sure the plant he wants to buy has a number at least as low.

2 | Lawn Planting

THE LAWN IS BOTH the background and foreground of a homesite. It directs the observer's eye to the house, and it must support and set off the house and the trees, shrubs, and flowers around it. A neglected lawn can ruin the appearance of a house; a well-kept lawn can sharpen up any rundown structure.

This crucial feature causes more frustration and anguish than any other element of home landscaping. Yet it is relatively easy to get a perfect lawn these days. Agricultural technology has developed dozens of good grass seeds for lawn turf. No matter where you live or what kind of soil you have, it is possible to produce a beautiful lawn.

In order to plant a grass turf that will give your yard a soft, green, lush, carpety look, you must first buy a seed that grows and thrives in your particular area, and one that is compatible with individual conditions of shade, drainage, and soil on your site.

Once the lawn is in, you must maintain it by proper mowing procedures and the best feeding methods. At the same time, you have to guard it against deterioration due to soil deficiencies, fungus diseases, insect infestations, and even the crushing assaults of weeds and crabgrass.

STEP-BY-STEP LAWN PLAN. Let's assume that you have moved into a brand-new suburban house standing pristine and alone on a hopelessly sterile lot that has been stripped of all growth—even of its topsoil. Proceed according to the outline below, a step-by-step plan, each point of which will be covered in detail following the outline.

(1) Determine the proper time to plant a new lawn in your particular area.

(2) Test the soil to see if its quality—acidity, composition, and fertility—will sustain a successful turf.

(3) Remove the topsoil and grade the land at subsoil level to get the proper drainage, pitch, and contour.

(4) Replace the original topsoil, if it is satisfactory; if not, apply new topsoil to a minimum depth of 4 to 6 inches all over.

(5) Alternately rake and roll the topsoil to get rid of all stones, debris, depressions, and humps.

(6) In accordance with the soil test in (2), add as much peat moss as is required—usually three to four bales per 1,000 square feet.

(7) Add superphosphate or bonemeal at the rate of 20 to 25 pounds per 1,000 square feet, if the soil test shows the need.

(8) Add lime, if the soil test shows the need.

(9) Fertilize with 20 to 30 pounds of plant food per 1,000 square feet to satisfy soil and seed requirements, as revealed by the soil test.

(10) Spread pest- and weed-control chemicals.

(11) Mix all these materials thoroughly into the topsoil.

(12) Select the proper seed, strain, or mix that is suitable to your particular area.

(13) Sow in the seed at the rate of 4 to 6 pounds per 1,000 square feet.

(14) Rake the seed in lightly.

(15) Roll the lawn so the seed is buried about $1/8$ inch deep.

(16) Mulch the new seedbed along the top to keep the seeds warm and prevent erosion of soil.

(17) Water the seedbed regularly until growth appears.

WHEN TO PLANT. Although local conditions vary around the country, the best time of the year to seed a new lawn is usually in the late summer and early fall, from about August 20 to October 10.

Seeds germinate best in the moist, cool weather of this period, allowing a new lawn to become established the following spring before the weeds begin to appear.

The next best time to seed a new lawn is in the early spring around April 20. However, you may have some difficulty preparing the ground for planting this early in the year. If so, you can seed a new lawn in May when the ground is usually easier to work.

TESTING TOPSOIL. In order to find out if you have a topsoil that will sustain a successful lawn turf, pick up a handful of dirt in your hand and squeeze it tightly. A quality soil will not form into a tight ball, but will fall apart as soon as you open your hand. If you're still not sure about it, drop a clump of dirt from your hand at about belt level. Good topsoil will fall apart before it hits the ground.

Quality topsoil, the kind you might buy for a new lawn, has a ratio of one part clay, one part silt, and one part sand. A soil equally balanced in this manner is called loam. Loam fortified with humus (organic matter) is ideal soil for growing plants. Such soil, as explained above, feels crumbly to the touch and is porous, with plenty of air space in between the soil particles. The soil is not necessarily black; in some areas the best topsoil is brown or red.

TOPSOIL ANALYSIS. No matter what quality of soil you have on your lot, you should make an analysis of it to find out how well it will support lawn grass and other plant life. A do-it-yourself soil analysis kit is available at your nearest garden store or a local university or county agricultural agent may be able to provide this service for a small fee. Briefly, soil analysis will show you: texture and structure, organic content, inorganic content, and pH reaction.

Texture and structure refer to the proportion of sand, silt, and clay that makes up the content of a soil.

Organic content includes decaying plant and animal matter, called *humus,* together with microorganisms and other forms of life that make the soil their home.

Inorganic content includes chemical elements present in a soil: nitrogen, phosphorous, potassium and others.

pH reaction means the degree of acidity or alkalinity in a soil. Very acid soils in moist regions have a pH of 4 or 5, while strongly alkaline soils in arid regions have a pH of 8 or 9. pH 7 is neutral, neither acid nor basic. Turf grasses thrive on the slightly acid side of neutrality, around pH 6. Most common lawn species flourish on soils as low as pH 5.5 to above 7.

A soil test will show you exactly how much of the following you need: superphosphate, lime, nitrogen and other elements like potassium and peat moss. It will also show you if you can get along with the soil you have, or if you need to buy a shipment of topsoil to insure a good lawn.

GRADING THE LAND. The first step in putting in a new lawn is to grade the surface of the ground so the grass will drain water away from the house and the grading will

In grading subsoil for a lawn on an irregularly sloped lot, plan to move fill materials like topsoil and extra dirt only one time. Remove all high spots first and push or wheel dirt to low spots until the slope is gentle and controlled. Then cover subsoil with 6 inches of topsoil.

FILL IN LOW SPOTS

TOP SOIL

REMOVE HIGH SPOTS

FILL IN LOW SPOTS

enable the grass turf to grow in easily. A drop of 1 foot in 50 should give you good steady drainage that will not erode the soil and that will keep the water moving away from the foundation.

In grading, you should first plan the exact level and profile of slope you want, and then remove all the topsoil already there and place it to one side.

If this task is too difficult to manage with a simple pick, shovel, and wheelbarrow, you can rent light earth-moving equipment from your nearest gardening store or power-tool rental. A small tractor with a bulldozer attachment should be sufficient to work the average suburban yard.

If you have severe slopes and different levels of land, you should consider constructing grass terraces, or possibly planting the severe slopes with ground cover.

We'll assume that you have no major earth-moving problems other than spreading topsoil or grading jobs that can be handled with a tractor and dozer.

LEVELING THE LAND. Move the topsoil to one side with hand tools or bulldozer and then level the entire subsoil area until it assumes the slope and contour that you want. Remove all rocks, bricks, and pieces of building debris that have become buried in the subsoil. Rake the subsoil to a smooth level either with a hand rake or with a rake attachment on a garden tractor.

If you have slightly different levels, awkward slopes, or humps in your grounds, try to round over all the sharp edges. It is difficult to mow a steep section of turf. Not only that, the grass itself will resist growing on a slant. Erosion will wash away most of the seeds and leave a bare area.

A slope steeper than 1 in 50 feet should be made as even as possible so you can water it and mow it without fear of wash-out or mowing accidents.

Level out all deep spots, too, so that pools of water will not form and rot the grass. Flatten out hillocks which might give you mowing trouble. A smooth, gradual, rounded curve is the profile you should strive for in any lawn-leveling job.

TOPSOIL. Once the subsoil is graded to your wishes, replace the old topsoil already removed from its surface, or cover the graded subsoil with new topsoil. In cases where the builder has stripped off all the topsoil, you should purchase a load of new topsoil.

If you do so, get the very best you can afford. It is ridiculous to buy cheap dirt, thinking you can replace it later with a better grade. You simply cannot pinch pennies and expect soil to improve all by itself.

You'll need a 4- to 6-inch layer of topsoil wherever you want a good lawn; if you purchase good topsoil, measure the volume you need and order it by the cubic yard.

Spread the topsoil and level it exactly as you leveled the subsoil.

PREPARATION OF SEEDBED. If your land is properly graded, and if you have the kind of topsoil you want, you need not bother with the preceding steps, but can start in with the preparation of the seedbed itself.

The best way to chop up the topsoil so that it is ready to receive plant food and seeds is to break it up with a rotary tiller, a power cultivator designed for garden areas. You can till with a fork, of course, but it's a hard job. Most modern gardeners use power to till. You can rent a power tiller from a garden-supply center. Chapter 12, Garden Tools, contains a thorough discussion of the rotary tiller.

The kind of dirt that will give you the best seedbed for grass planting will consist of particles of soil varying from the size of a pea to the size of a golfball. This concentration of dirt will give the seeds plenty of places to lodge and be sheltered from the sun and wind.

After breaking up the dirt with the rotary tiller, be sure to alternately rake and roll the topsoil to get rid of all stones, debris, depressions and humps, leaving the loam loose enough to take the seeds.

Deere & Company

Most modern homeowners use gas-powered tillers like this one to turn soil. Tiller can be rented from a garden-supply center. Without tilling, most soil cannot be used properly either for grass or plants.

FEEDING THE SOIL. After you have spread the topsoil evenly, and have tilled it to the proper consistency for a lawn seedbed, you should consider the addition of such soil enrichers as peat moss, superphosphate, lime, and nitrogen.

You can build a lawn without peat moss, and you may get a fine turf that will stand up. But if you live in an area where there is liable to be drought or very hot days, you should consider the application of peat moss to retain moisture in the soil.

Peat moss. This is an important addition to a soil that has either high clay or high sand content. High-clay soil is not sufficiently loose to allow moisture and air to penetrate; sandy soil is unable to retain moisture and air to nourish the roots.

If the soil test shows you have topsoil with high clay or high sand content, you should add peat moss to it; its presence will loosen clayey soil and help retain moisture in sandy soil.

For each 1,000 square feet of lawn area, add from three to four bales of peat moss —coarse-grade sphagnum peat is the best—or one or more cubic yards of substitutes: compost; rotted manure; rotted sawdust; leaf mold; sewage sludge; or some other processed organic. A covering of about 1 inch of this material over the surface is required.

Superphosphate. A second material your soil analysis may indicate a need for is superphosphate. If your lawn area is well protected from running feet and other heavy traffic, you may be able to ignore the addition of superphosphate.

However, if you want to protect your lawn from walking feet, running shoes, and action sports, add in about 20 to 25 pounds of superphosphate per 1,000 square feet of lawn. It will provide a rugged turf by promoting a deep root system in the grass. Adding an equal amount of bonemeal will give you equally good results.

Typical mechanical spreader designed to introduce fertilizer, lime, and seed onto lawn plot is pushed from behind by operator.

D. M. Scott & Sons Co.

Fertilizer or seed should be spread with a definite pattern in mind. Avoid overlaps if possible. Make all turns with spreader closed so as not to doublefeed any areas. When seeding, keep walking evenly and at a steady speed.

Lime. If your soil test shows that you need lime, add it in at the rate recommended by the analysis. Do not add lime until the soil test is made. If you overlime a lawn you will encourage the future growth of crabgrass.

Fertilizer. Almost any soil test will show that you need a "complete" fertilizer to grow grass seed. A complete fertilizer is a mix that contains the three major elements necessary for lawn growth: nitrogen, phosphorous, and potassium. One typical ratio of these chemical elements is a mix of 10-6-4; other mixes are available for almost every kind of soil condition possible.

The first number refers to the amount in pounds in a 100-pound bag of nitrogen; the second number refers to the amount in pounds in a 100-pound bag of phosphorus; and the third number to the amount in pounds of potassium.

You should spread this complete fertilizer at the rate of 25 pounds per 1,000 square feet when laying in a new lawn. A discussion with your local garden store expert will give you the correct formula for your soil and climate.

Chapter 3, How to Maintain a Lawn, includes a discussion of using fertilizers for lawn maintenance.

Pest and weed control. You should also put down insecticides and herbicides to keep grubs and other pests in control, along with weeds like crabgrass. Consult your local lawn expert, or agricultural agent, for any special recommendations for your area. Insecticides and herbicides are poisonous; you should know how to protect pets, children, and the soil itself from them.

WORKING IN PRE-SOWING MATERIALS. All these pre-sowing materials – peat moss, superphosphate, lime, complete fertilizer, and pest- and weed-controls – should be spread on in an even layer over the soil. Then you should work them into the soil thoroughly by using a rotary tiller or a hand rake.

Spreading these materials uniformly over the lawn site is of course essential to good turf growth. Hand spreaders and power spreaders are available for such work, covered in Chapter 12, Garden Tools.

After tilling, rake the seedbed level, but do not roll it yet. You'll find it easier to plant seed on a slightly rough bed, with chunks of soil the size described under "Seedbed Preparation."

Soak the soil thoroughly and let it dry out for a day or two before sowing the seed.

SELECTING THE RIGHT GRASS SEED. There is a proper grass seed for your particular lawn, for your neighborhood, and for your geographic area. A discussion at the end of this chapter will show you the types of grass seed available, with an explanation of growth habits and appearance of each.

Compare the strains listed with what is available at your local stores, and discuss grass types with your neighbors. You'll be surprised sometimes at what you learn about seeds that won't grow and seeds that will.

When it comes to deciding the right kind of grass or grass mix to use, don't forget that an expensive, fine-textured grass will give you much more extensive yield than a coarse-textured cheap grass. Even though you pay more for the seed itself, you'll get your money's worth in a much better lawn.

SOWING THE SEED. You can sow grass seed in two ways: by hand or with a spreader.

If you sow by hand, mix the seed with an equal volume of fine sand or sifted soil to give the mass bulk. Do not sow in the wind. Wait until the air is still, and scatter the seed in wide arcs, walking first in parallel lines one way, and then at right angles again over the same area.

If you sow with a seeder or spreader, divide the total amount of seed into two parts, and apply half in one direction, and the second half at right angles to the first half. The idea is to get uniform seeding.

You will probably get better seeding by using a mechanical spreader. The correct setting for the spreader calibration is always indicated on the package of grass seed. Simply set the spreader to that number, and sow the grass uniformly.

There are also power seeders that broadcast the seeds over a wider area at each pass than regular mechanical spreaders. See Chapter 12, Garden Tools.

When you are finished spreading, you should find that about twelve or fifteen seeds cover a square inch of ground – an adequate number for a good stand of grass.

Use from 4 to 6 pounds of seed per 1,000 square feet. The correct rate varies from seed to seed or mix to mix. The average rate will give you a good grass cover that will

Cyclone Seeder Co., Inc.

Seed can be spread by hand, as shown at left or a mechanical seeder can be pushed along as at right. Mechanical seeder does a more uniform job.

tend to keep out weeds and produce a better turf than a lighter amount will.

Set aside about half a pound of seed for every 1,000 square feet for patching after the first mowing.

RAKING THE SEEDS IN. After sowing the seed, rake it lightly into the soil with a flexible rake, pulling the rake toward you.

Mix the seeds in the upper quarter-inch of soil, making sure you cover the seed with no more than one-eighth inch of dirt. If the seed is too deep, it will not germinate.

Once you have the seeds under one-eighth inch of soil, give the area a thorough but gentle watering, using a sprinkler that gives a fine, mist-like spray.

ROLLING THE LAWN. When the seed is buried properly to a depth of about one-eighth inch, roll the entire lawn area with a hand roller or a roller attachment on a garden tractor. Use the size and weight roller recommended by your garden store. Too heavy a roller will impact the earth; too light a roller will allow the seeds to work up to the surface in the lightest rain.

MULCHING THE SEEDBED. The purpose of mulching, or laying a protective covering over a newly planted lawn area, is to speed up germination of the grass seeds by keeping the ground moist and warm. Without mulch, soil may dry out and crack. Mulching also prevents soil and seeds from eroding down slopes when watered or rained on.

There are many materials you can use for lawn mulch: straw, hay, sphagnum moss, compost, wood chips (never sawdust!), or paper or cloth. If you use straw or hay, spread about one bale over 1,000 square feet of lawn. Leave the mulch on and let it disintegrate. When you can't see the straw or hay anymore, it's time to cut the new grass.

Slopes or terraced sections of a newly planted lawn present special problems to the home owner because of the tendency of loose soil and new seeds to erode away when watered or when rained on. Special mulching can keep the soil in place and stimulate growth of the newly planted seeds.

Ordinary types of mulch like compost and hay cannot be used in this situation to good effect, however. Cheesecloth, netting, or mulching paper is the best available material.

Polyethylene paper sold commercially by garden supply stores is excellent for this type of slope mulching. Before laying the polyethylene down, water the entire seeded area. Cover all seeded soil with the plastic paper, fastening it to the ground with stakes or wires.

The plastic paper will keep warmth in the seeded area just above ground level, and tend to prevent moisture from escaping into the air by natural evaporation. The moisture and warmth will enhance the growth of the grass seedlings.

Each time you water, remove the plastic sheets and then replace them carefully. As soon as the first blades of grass appear, take up the plastic paper. The new grass will now be able to hold its own against erosion action.

WATERING THE SEEDBED. You should water the newly sown seedbed daily, or even twice a day on sunny or windy days, to keep the soil moist but not flooded. Water at midday and evening; at 10 a.m. and 5 p.m.; or at 1 p.m. and 5 p.m. Set your watering pattern so you won't do any walking over the newly sown area.

You can reduce the watering frequency gradually as seedling grasses begin to shade the ground and protect the new ones. However, once germination begins, continue to keep the soil moist. Do not put down too much water—just spray the ground lightly and often.

Watering is done best by a mechanical sprinkler that gives the lawn uniform moisture over all its area.

GRASS SEEDS AVAILABLE. In the United States, there are roughly three different kinds of grass seeds: cool-season seeds; warm-season seeds; and extreme-season seeds. The first two are the most important; the third is a combination of the other two and can sometimes be replaced by them.

Cool-season grasses grow best in areas of moderate climates located in the northern parts of the country, where the soil temperature generally remains about 80 degrees F. This growing area extends north from the Ohio River Valley. In this region, the grass grows and appears best in the spring and autumn. South from Tennessee, the grass tends to be a bit weak. In hot, dry spells, it lies dormant, and is a constant prey to crabgrass. Grasses in this region are mostly planted from seeds.

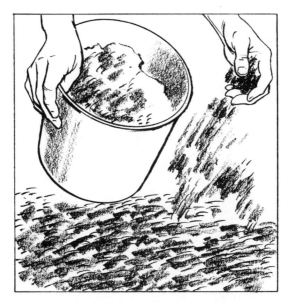

The simplest way to spread mulch on a new seedbed is to sow it by hand (above). Follow directions for whatever type of commercial mulch used. For lawn sowed on slope (below), lay mulching cloth or polyethylene plastic mulch paper over newly planted grass to keep it from eroding. Leave cover on until first grass appears.

Warm-season grasses grow best in areas of warm climate located in the southern parts of the country, where the soil temperature generally remains about 90 degrees. In this region, when the temperature sinks too far downward, the grass tends to go dormant and changes color to brown. This growing area extends south from Tennessee, through southeast Virginia, through the Coastal Plains and from Florida to Eastern Texas, and on to the West Coast. The grasses in this region are mostly planted from live starts: sprigs and plugs.

Extreme-season seeds grow best in areas of extreme climate: warm and cold; wet and dry. High elevations in these areas generally favor cool-season grasses, and lowlands are more suitable to warm-season grasses.

The kind of grass you choose for your lawn will depend on these considerations: geographic location, climatic extremes, soil conditions, and sunlight and shade.

COOL-SEASON GRASSES. In the Northeast, in parts of the Midwest, and in the northern West Coast regions, five main types of cool-season grasses can usually be grown with moderate success:

(1) Kentucky bluegrass
(2) Red fescue
(3) Creeping bentgrass
(4) Italian ryegrass
(5) Redtop

Kentucky bluegrass *(Pos pratensis)*. The most popular and successful of all the cool-season grasses is called common Kentucky bluegrass. Its brilliant, dark-green color and boat-shaped leaf tips help make a beautiful, close-knit turf that grows on sandy loams and on clay soils as well. Its endurance and density of growth make it excellent for lawns in the humid cool regions of North America, including the Pacific Northwest, and throughout much of the northern and central Great Plains and intermountain area.

All strains of Kentucky bluegrass have well-developed rhizomes, which are underground stems that help produce a tough sod. Bluegrass loves the sun and does not grow well in shade, except in the South where it will live only in moderate shade.

Mowing at less than 1½ inches will hamper underground root stalk development. Bluegrass is best adapted to well-drained, productive soils of some limestone origin.

Bluegrass is susceptible to leaf spot, if grown on poorly drained soils, or if it is overirrigated, but it will survive most pest invasions. It has a high tolerance of drought and moderately alkaline soils, but not much tolerance of very acid soils. It may lie doggo in hot, dry weather, but it will start to green up again when the weather permits.

The seed takes two to three weeks to germinate and it requires a full growing season to form its turf.

Five main derivatives of Kentucky bluegrass are most commonly used: Merion, Windsor, Newport, Park and Prato.

Sow: 2-4/M (2-4 pounds of seed to 1,000 square feet of lawn.) *Mow:* 1½" or higher, usually rotary mower.

Merion bluegrass. Merion, the most popular derivative of Kentucky bluegrass, produces a fine turf if it gets full sunlight in a slightly acid soil of about pH 6.5, (see section on Topsoil Analysis earlier in this chapter) producing good color, short leaves, and low growth.

Merion needs heavy feeding and plenty of watering. However, it is highly resistant to leaf spot, a fungus disease, although it is susceptible to rust and powdery mildew.

It requires twice as much nitrogen as common Kentucky bluegrass because of its vigorous growth. Remove all clippings each time you mow Merion. It is also important not to allow thatch – plant debris like clipped grass and leaves – to accumulate on the ground surface; remove them by raking or by use of power dethatchers.

Merion is susceptible to winter injury.

It is resistant to drought, and intolerant to close mowing. Merion requires regular cutting and maintenance.

Sow: 2/M. *Mow:* 1½", reel or rotary motor.

Windsor bluegrass. Another Kentucky bluegrass variety in considerable supply is Windsor, which costs more than Merion, but which grows well in high summer heat and in low-nitrogen soils without yellowing. It is moderately resistant to leaf spot.

Sow/Mow: Same as above for Kentucky bluegrass.

Park bluegrass. Park, a variety of Kentucky bluegrass, represents a mixture of several selections of blue. In Minnesota it is described as superior to Merion in seedling and plant vigor, resistant to rust, and sod formation.

Sow/Mow: Same as above for Kentucky bluegrass.

Newport bluegrass. The Newport variety of bluegrass comes from and grows in the Pacific Northwest. It is vigorous, highly productive, and tolerant of that climate. Newport features a moderately broad hard, low-growing green leaf, sturdiness in the fall months, speed in sod formation, and a fairly good resistance to rust and leaf spot.

However, Newport does not wear well. As the years roll by, it sometimes thins out and begins to look ragged and sparse.

Sow/Mow: Same as above for Kentucky bluegrass.

Prato bluegrass. Another type of bluegrass is Prato, a derivative that forms a dense, fine-textured turf. Each plant is leafy, with medium-wide, short leaves. Prato will tolerate a rather close mowing height, and is moderately resistant to leaf spot and rust.

Sow-Mow: Same as above for Kentucky bluegrass.

Other varieties of Kentucky bluegrass include: Arboretum, Beltsville 117-27(6), Belturf, Delta, K5(47), Nu Dwarf, P-4358, and Troy.

Mixed bluegrass. The real beauty of Kentucky bluegrass is that it can be used with many other types of grass as the base of a mix.

If purchasing a mix, you should make sure that there is at least a 45 per cent amount of Kentucky bluegrass present.

Don't forget, bluegrass is slow in germinating. It rarely shows up at all sooner than three weeks after sowing.

You can buy "shade" mixtures of bluegrass, which means that there is a little "rough bluegrass" mixed in with Kentucky. A special grass called *Poa trivialis* is usually mixed in with "shade" mixes.

Sow/Mow: Same as above for Kentucky bluegrass.

Rough bluegrass *(Poa trivialis).* Rough bluegrass is light green in color and it prefers moist, cool conditions that are often present in shady exposures. Like its cousin Kentucky bluegrass, it greens up early in the spring and stays green late into the fall.

Because *Poa*'s leaves are soft, it won't stand up too well to heavy traffic. However, if you mow it at a low height and keep it constantly watered, it will come through extremely well in hot periods.

Sow: 3/M. *Mow:* 1½" or higher, usually rotary mower.

Red fescue *(Festuca rubra)*. A good thick-turfed, sod-forming shade grass for lawns in the cool-season regions is red fescue, a grass that is tolerant of drought, shade, and cold, of sandy, dry or acid soil, and can thrive under considerable neglect.

Fescue doesn't do well if it's fertilized with too much nitrogen, and it doesn't like pest-control chemicals, especially those emulsified in oil.

Its fine, dark-green, needle-like leaves, rather stiff and wiry, grow rolled tightly together. The tightness of growth captures the moisture, and is one reason fescue is drought-resistant.

Fescue has underground root stalks, and a creeping habit of growth. It makes a good, thick sod, and neither shade nor drought cuts down on the turf quality or density.

Fescue does best in a soil of about pH 6, although it can stand more acidity. If mixed with bluegrass, fescue should compose about 40 per cent of the total.

Do not overwater fescue. It's a lazy man's grass; don't give it too much care or the growth will wither away.

Several varieties of red fescue include Clatsop, Duraturf, Illahee, Olds, Pennlawn, Rainier, and Rhode Island 6.

Sow: 3-5/M. *Mow:* 1½″ or higher, usually rotary mower.

Creeping bentgrass *(Agrostis palustris)*. Creeping bentgrass grows best under intensive irrigation, although it is actually moderately drought-resistant. It thrives in wet areas like the Pacific Northwest.

Growing above the ground on runners, or stolons, like a strawberry plant, creeping bentgrass has an excellent texture, makes a fine greensward, and under optimum conditions of moisture and warmth the seed germinates in a week to form a thick turf within a few months.

It requires frequent mowing, topdressing, and thinning. Without attention, it will go bad. Grown alone, bentgrass is susceptible to diseases, but in mixes, it is relatively immune to them. It is not a high-standing grass, and is tolerant of acid and alkaline soils.

Varieties of creeping bentgrass include Arlington, C-52, Cohansey, Collins, Congressional, Dahlgren, Evansville, Metropolitan, Norbeck, Pencross, Pennlu, Seaside, Toronto, and Washington.

Sow: 2-3/M. *Mow:* ½-1″, reel mower with extra blades.

Italian ryegrass *(Lolium multiflorum)*. Italian ryegrass is a major annual grass grown principally in the Pacific Coast states west of the Cascades and as a winter annual in the South. Ryegrass germinates rapidly, and offers protection and erosion control to the slower perennial grasses that take longer to grow.

Watch out for too great a quantity of annual ryegrass in a grass mix; you will end up with bare spots in the lawn after a cold winter. And look out for a seed mixture that boasts more than 20 per cent Italian rye.

Varieties of Italian ryegrass include Astor, Florida Rust-Resistant, Gulf, H-1, La Estanzuela 284, Ryegrass 12, Stoneville Rust-Resistant Strains, Tifton 1, and Wimmera 62.

Perennial ryegrass *(Lolium perenne)*. This grass is less coarse than the annual ryegrasses, and is an important cool-season bunchgrass. It sprouts quickly and grows reasonably well, doing best in heavy soils, in cool, moist regions with mild winters. It is not quite so durable nor does it knit so tight a sod as Kentucky bluegrass.

Sow: 6-8M. *Mow:* 1½″ or higher, reel or rotary mower.

Redtop *(Agrostis alba)*. This annual or perennial is a coarse grass that sometimes turns clumpy with age. It is actually a rough bentgrass, fairly light green in color, undemanding and widely adaptable for use on poorly drained acid soils. Because its mixtures generally contain weed seeds, it is apt to turn coarse and weedy. It is best used as a temporary grass in lawn seed mixtures.

Sow: 2/M. Mow: 1″ or more, reel or rotary mower.

WARM-SEASON GRASSES. Throughout the south-central states, some of the Southwest, and throughout the South as described before in more detail, four types of warm-season grasses are usually grown with success:

(1) Bermuda grass
(2) St. Augustine grass
(3) Japanese lawngrass
(4) Manila grass.

Bermuda grass *(Cynodon)*. The most important of all the warm-season grasses is Bermuda grass. A deep-rooted, sod-forming grass, tolerant to drought and tolerant to saline conditions, it grows rampant in sunshine, but doesn't wither in shade. It grows in the South and Southwest most successfully.

Bermuda grass needs lots of nitrogen for optimum growth, along with a neutral or slightly acid soil, up to six feedings a year, and frequent mowing.

Since it grows above ground by runners and below ground by rhizomes, it is difficult to confine and requires lots of edging and cutting back. It can become a pest in a flower garden, under a hedge, or in a cultivated area.

Bermuda grass needs frequent mowing, frequent fertilization, and frequent removal of clippings from the lawn. It grows best in temperatures of 75 degrees or higher. If you don't have that much warmth, don't expect Bermuda grass to grow at all.

Sow: 2-3/M. Mow: 1″ or less. (Some Bermuda grass is started by sprigs or plugs.)

Many varieties of Bermuda grass are available: Bayshore, Coastal, Everglades, Greenfield, Midland, NK-37, Ormond, Royal Cape, Sunturf, Suwannee, Texturf 1F, Texturf 10, Tiffine, Tifgreen, Tiflawn, Tifway, Tufcote, U-3, and Uganda.

U-3, the oldest variety of hybrid Bermuda grass, has a fair tolerance of frost and low temperatures. It is grown in the more northerly regions of the South. U-3 is coarser than some of the newer varieties.

Tifgreen is a disease-resistant type of Bermuda grass used in very fine home lawns. Rapid-spreading, producing a double turf, it can be adapted to use for putting greens because of its sturdiness.

Tiflawn spreads fast, makes dense and fine turf.

Ormond, usually grown in the Deep South and in Southern California, is a dark-green grass that will retain full color until the autumn. It is resistant to certain leaf-spot diseases, but is susceptible to dollar spot.

Tifway, dark green, frost-resistant, sod webworm and mole cricket resistant, can be mixed with Tiflawn to form a good turf.

Sunturf, a perennial, is fine-leaved, dark green, with low growth, and rapid spread. Drought-resistant, it is susceptible to rust.

St. Augustine grass *(Stenotaphrum secundatum)*. A good selection for lawn turf in the mild areas of the East Coast westward to eastern Texas is St. Augustine grass. Coarse in texture, with a dark-green color, it excels in sod formation and in tolerance to salt spray, but must be irrigated constantly in dry weather, and grows best on relatively fertile, well-drained soils.

It will survive cold weather and shade, yet is susceptible to chinch-bug invasions.

With St. Augustine grass you should not use herbicides of the 2,4-D or 2,4,5-TP variety, either.

Yet if you protect the grass, it will give you an attractive cover of a somewhat coarse texture that requires little mowing or attention.

Plant: from sod, sprigs, or plugs. *Mow:* 1½″, rotary or reel, average frequency.

Bahia grass *(Paspalum notatum flugge).* Bahia grass is a major warm-season grass that grows slowly by short stolons. It is an aggressive species that spreads rapidly from seed, and is well-suited for use on sandy soils of low fertility where good fertilizer programs are not maintained. It grows in Florida, and the lower Coastal Plains.

Varieties of Bahia grass include Argentina, Paraguay, Paraguay 22, Pensacola, Pensacola X Common, Tifhi 1, Tifhi 2, and Wilmington.

Sow: 4/M. *Mow:* 1½-2″, rotary or reel mower.

Centipede grass *(Eremochloa ophiuroides).* A good sod-forming grass that has come to the South from China is centipede grass. This variety grows on poor soils, and is well adapted to climatic and soil conditions of the South. It is a low-maintenance, general-purpose lawn grass.

Sow: seeds. *Plant:* sprigs or plugs. *Mow:* reel or rotary mower.

Japanese lawngrass *(Zoysia japonica).* The elite of the Southern grasses, especially in the zones near the north, is Japanese lawngrass, popularly known by its Latin name, zoysia, a native sod-forming grass from Asia.

This grass has a root system that forms a dense sod of narrow-bladed, grayish-green turf. It spreads the same way that Bermuda grass does, laterally by rhizomes and stolons. It is resistant to wear, but recovers slowly when really damaged, and must have full exposure to the sun to survive.

Zoysia is drought-resistant, crowds out crabgrass and other weeds — especially the broadleaf varieties — and will grow in almost any soil available, the poorer the better. It grows best in heavy soils. This grass is not drought-resistant, nor does it thrive where summers are short or cool.

It has a very slow start, and an even slower spread. It takes two years or more to form a satisfactory sod, depending on soil, climate and planting practices.

The transplanting of zoysia is critical. You must coddle it like a baby during the first week. Then it takes about twenty-one days to recover and start spreading.

Zoysia is about as much a lazy man's grass as Manila grass (see below), once it gets growing. You'll only have to mow it when you feel like it. Make sure when you do that the mower is sharp.

It will be green in May and brown in October. It does not tolerate shade when grown in the North.

Varieties include Beltsville selection, Meyer (medium grade), Midwest (coarse grade), Emerald (fine grade), and 2-73.

Sow: seeds. *Plant:* sprigs and plugs. *Mow:* 1-2″, heavy-duty mower.

Manila grass *(Zoysia matrella).* Resistant to insects and diseases, immune to salt spray and foot traffic damage, Manila grass will grow in full sun or in partial shade and will develop a four-inch thick mat of turf strong enough to strangle weeds. It has a dark green color that stays all through autumn, with finer, denser sod than *Zoysia japonica,* although it is less hardy.

However, a period of two years is sometimes required before a really thick turf develops. These first two years are the critical period for any Manila grass. You'll have to give it a lot of water, frequent feedings, and many weedings. But when it finally grows in, your hard work is rewarded with a good-looking, rugged grass.

It grows in the southwestern United States, where it is used as a lawn grass.

EXTREME-SEASON GRASSES. The transitional region between warm-season grass and cool-season grass includes parts of Colorado, Wyoming, Montana, California, Kansas, Nevada, Nebraska, the Dakotas, Oregon, Washington, Texas, Utah, and Oklahoma, where certain areas of violent extremes of heat and cold, of wet and dry weather, make ordinary lawns difficult to maintain.

For these in-between regions, certain lawn grasses flourish:
(1) Buffalo grass
(2) Blue grama
(3) Crested wheatgrass
(4) *Dichondra repens.*
(NOTE: Kentucky bluegrass and fescue, cool-season grasses, may be successfully grown in these regions, but they must be planted as sod during the late summer or early fall, or early spring. Warm-season grasses should be planted as sprigs or plugs in late spring or early summer.)

Buffalo grass *(Büchloe dactyloides).* A native perennial, buffalo grass is actually a warm-season, sod-forming grass that spreads by stolons. It occurs mainly in the Great Plains. Drought-resistant, it requires infrequent mowing and can take very bad weather. You should seed buffalo grass in April or early May, or sod only female plants (male plants produce weird flowers that do not look right in a lawn). Seed and sod on moist soil. Plug buffalo grass from mid-May to June if you can keep the weeds under control and the grass well-watered until the lawn comes in.

Blue grama *(Bouteloua gracilis).* A major warm-season native grass in the Great Plains, blue grama is used mainly for erosion control, but can also serve in lawns. It has a creeping growth habit, and forms dense sod that produces high-quality grass that is hardy and resistant to drought. It grows in many different types of ground, but prefers heavy, rolling upland soils.

Various varieties include Lovington, and the Woodward Strains (over a dozen). Other strains of grama, including black grama, sideoats grama, and hairy grama, grow in many parts of the Great Plains and the West.

Crested wheatgrass *(Agropyron desertorum).* A major cool-season bunchgrass originally from Siberia, crested wheatgrass does well in the northern Great Plains, and even in the Sierra Nevada Mountains and south to northern Arizona and New Mexico. This important grass is actually used for pasture, hay, and erosion-control. It is drought-resistant, long-lived, but will not withstand too much flooding.

It starts growth in the early spring before the native grasses. Although it goes dormant and brown in extremes of heat, it otherwise does very well for lawns.

Varieties include Mandan 2194B, Mandan 2359, Nebraska 10, Nordan, South Dakota 15, Summit, Summit 62, and Utah 42-1.

HOW TO "SOD" A LAWN. If it is not practicable for you to lay in a new lawn, and if you want an "instant" lawn no matter how high the cost, you may find that sodding will be the answer to your problem.

Sod can be purchased from a lawn or garden store. It is delivered rolled up like a carpet in strips anywhere from 12 to 18 inches wide. After clearing the area where sod is to be laid, simply unroll strips, butting them tightly to one another. Fill in cracks with topsoil. When sod is laid, water and treat like grass.

Sodding solves another persistent dilemma: the production of a good lawn on slopes steeper than the 1 in 50 feet mentioned as preferred for a successful lawn. Sodding may also be the solution to other types of areas that are difficult to seed.

When you shop for sod, shop for it exactly as you would for a new grass seed. The grass itself will not improve with age; it will remain exactly the same as the grass you first see in the sod samples. You should be able to get a guarantee not only as to the *grass* in the sample, but also as to the *soil* in the sod.

(1) When you lay in sod, prepare the ground exactly as you would for seeding. Then water the sod so that it is moist before you lay it in.

(2) Once you lay in the sod, water it again so that sod and soil underneath will both be wet.

(3) Sod at least ¾ of an inch to an inch thick will give you the quickest binding with a soil base.

(4) Lay the sod strips the same way you would lay a carpet on a floor. Fill in the small areas between the strips or squares with moist topsoil, making sure that there are no weeds or weed seeds in it.

(5) Press the strips of sod into the earth with a flat board.

(6) Commercial strips of sodding are carefully cut so that the depth will be uniform throughout the roll. However, you may find that the grass humps up at one point and sags at another. Roll the sod back and work in a little soil fill under the low spots, and cut down the high spots. Then lay the sod again to be sure it is even on top. With the moist earth easily workable, you should have no trouble evening out the wrinkles.

3 | How to Maintain a Lawn

ONCE YOU HAVE ESTABLISHED an attractive lawn you must maintain it. Grass is an aggressive grower, and if given a chance to thrive will successfully compete with all other plants including the most robust of weeds. Often, however, the grass simply does not get an equal chance to compete – particularly if it is not maintained correctly.

Good maintenance of grass consists of four main points, and several subordinate points. Of greatest importance are:

(1) Grass should be mowed regularly with a sharp mower set to cut at about 1½ inches on the average.

(2) Grass should be watered regularly where the weather is hot and dry.

(3) Lawn turf should be fertilized at least three times a year with the proper kind of plant food.

(4) If a soil test shows lack of lime, you should apply lime regularly to the turf loam.

The majority of turf failures can generally be traced to the failure of the lawn owner to pursue these four ends. In some cases, however, there are several other points to be observed:

(5) Compacted areas of grass should be aerated by special tools to keep the grass growing.

(6) Bare patches of turf must be seeded immediately in order to keep weeds from taking over.

(7) Certain rare occasions demand rolling of grass even after it has grown up.

(8) Lawn weeds and insect pests should be eliminated by application of chemicals to the lawn.

Let's take a look first at the primary concern in lawn care – mowing.

HOW TO MOW AN ESTABLISHED LAWN. Next to the actual planting and care of grass seed before it germinates, the mowing and trimming of a lawn is the most important part of turf maintenance.

If a lawn is not cut enough, it grows too thick, and then begins to thin itself out. If the grass is too high when first cut, it will turn brown for several days and the cut-off tops will retard the growth of new grass.

If the lawn is cut too much, it will not be able to grow fully and strongly. For that reason, it will tend to be more easily crowded out by weeds.

Except on certain kinds of bentgrass and Bermuda grass lawn, set your mower to cut at about 1½ inches from the ground. Keep the mower set at that height throughout the spring and summer until all growth stops in the fall. Regular mowing at this height will give you the most healthy and vigorous lawn turf possible.

Direction of cut. Vary the direction of your mowing attack on the lawn by alternating it from week to week. For instance, if you cut the lawn lengthwise today, cut it crosswise next week, and diagonally the week after. Variety will give the turf a well-groomed appearance.

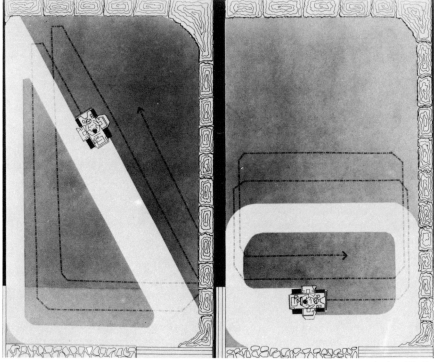

Jacobsen Mfg. Co.

To eliminate unnecessary backing and turning when mowing a lawn, plan to follow a continuous mowing pattern. Experts feel that alternating mowing patterns every cutting will give a smoother look and eliminate wheel markings. Plan at left shows a diagonal pattern that moves across the yard in a triangular design. Plan at right uses a rectangular design.

Certain lawns are best cut by attacking the borders first, then working in from the borders to the exact center of the lawn. If you use this method — usually more suitable for a lawn area without any trees, shrubs, or garden plots — you can vary the cut by starting at the center the next week and working outward in squares to the borders.

What to do with clippings. Argument has raged for years over what to do with lawn clippings: let them lie on the lawn and return naturally to the soil? Or pick them up in a catcher and let them rot in a compost heap?

Ecological studies have turned up the interesting fact that lawn clippings should be recycled much as other elements in nature; in other words, you should collect them as you mow, and consign them to the compost pile.

Composting causes bacterial action to dispose of the clippings and return them to elemental chemicals and organic waste faster than they would lying on the lawn.

Aside from practicing good ecology, collecting grass clippings will prevent them from accumulating and forming thatch at the point where grass blades emerge from the soil. Thatch can strangle grass growth as well as prevent moisture and air from mixing in with the soil.

Turf maintenance technicians recommend using a grass catcher on a power mower so cuttings can be recycled in compost heap. Compost mulch will return organic nutriments to soil, eliminating need for other fertilizers. Empty clippings onto a large tarpaulin and carry to compost heap.

Jacobsen Mfg. Co.

Composting prevents the spread of fungus disease that has attacked grass blades, too; the clippings will confine the fungus to the compost heap where it will join bacterial action in breaking down the organic matter to its elements.

Edging and trimming. Edging and trimming are as important in the maintenance of a lawn as the initial mowing itself.

Edging refers to the cutting of grass blades that grow at the outside perimeter of the lawn, usually where walks, driveways, and patio slabs meet the turf.

The easiest way to edge a lawn is by using a power edger that does the job as you push it along. A power edger usually has a blade in a vertical position and shears off the grass in a straight line at the junction of turf and walkway.

Trimming resembles edging, and refers to the part of cleaning up that takes place where the lawn meets natural obstructions—rocks surrounding a tree trunk, stone walls, garden areas, planters, and so on.

The easiest way to trim a lawn is to use a power edger-trimmer that combines edging and trimming in one simple operation.

If you do not use a power edger and/or trimmer, you'll have to do the job by hand with a hand trimmer. There are, incidentally, hand-held battery-operated edgers that do a fine job.

How often should you mow? How frequently you should mow depends upon the kind of grass you have and its rate of growth during any one period. Do not mow because a certain number of days have elapsed; mow because a certain amount of growth has been observed. To get maximum-strength turf, mow to remove as little of the green area of the grass leaf as possible. It is the green part visible that assimilates food for growth.

Most families find each weekend the natural time to mow. Through most of the growing season, grass is a little more than ready for mowing every seven days.

You can reasonably compromise between a once-a-week schedule and an ideal frequency by following this old rule of thumb: "Never remove more grass than you leave."

Disston Corp.

Trimming against walls or borders can be difficult job for mower. Here battery-activated hand-held grass shears reduce trimming time needed with ordinary shears and take edge off fatigue.

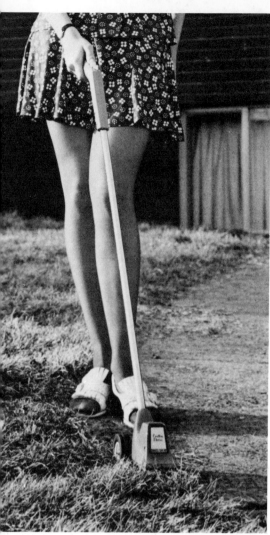

Jacobsen Mfg. Co.

Disston Corp.

Special battery-activated upright grass shears help perform edging chores along walks and driveways, permitting operator to work without bending over.

Power edge-trimmer does job of edging and trimming, saving time and energy on fairly large piece of suburban property.

If the grass is maintained at 1 inch, you should cut it before it reaches 2 inches. If you are growing at 1½ inches, mow before it grows to 3 inches.

If you let the grass grow too high between mowings, the high blades will shade and brown out the lower leaves. Then, when you cut the tall growth, the lawn will go brown and look scalped.

MOWING EQUIPMENT. There are so many different kinds of lawn-mowing machines that it would be impossible to list them all here. However, there are several kinds that you should be familiar with.

To begin with, there are reel mowers and rotary mowers. Reel mowers were familiar in the "good old days," when almost everyone had to push his lawn mower across the grass. Most hand-pushed mowers that do not operate on power are of this variety.

However, there are power mowers with reel blades, particularly those large ones that are used to cut grass along freeways and in large areas of open land.

The rotary-type blade is mounted at a certain height from the ground; it revolves constantly at that one level, cutting all grass it comes into contact with. By pushing the machine forward, you cut the grass at a uniform level.

A reel mower has these advantages:

(1) It gives a velvety, smooth cut; however, the lawn must be even and flat and mowed regularly.

(2) It cuts Kentucky bluegrass and similar species well, but it is a poor performer when it comes to cutting bunch-type grasses.

(3) It gives the best service in cutting a formal or semiformal lawn.

A rotary mower has these advantages:

(1) It cuts *any* lawn, no matter how bumpy the ground, how uneven the grass or clumpy the turf.

(2) It mows *any* kind of grass and cuts and trims weeds and other vegetation too high for reel mowers.

(3) It pulverizes leaves, returning valuable organic matter to the soil.

(4) Its blades are easy to take off and sharpen with a file.

Rotary mowers come in many different shapes and sizes, their designs geared to the varieties of lawns they must cut. Almost all rotary mowers are power mowers, the cutting blades whirling independent of the operator's thrust.

The size of the lawn determines the width of cut and the horsepower of a rotary power mower; the various obstacles and constructions encountered on the lawn determines the maneuverability of the machine.

Power mowers can be either hand-pushed or self-propelled. In both types the cutting blades are power-driven. The self-propelled mower has a clutch that when engaged operates the wheels to pull the unit along. The self-propelled mower is ideal for large expanses of grass and steep slopes.

The largest of the self-propelled mowers is a riding mower, equipped with a saddle seat; it looks like a small garden tractor. Other larger rigs include a separate tractor that pulls lawn-garden attachments behind it.

The most common kind of power mower in use is the hand-propelled walk-behind rotary power model. Popular cutting widths run from about 18 to 22 inches, with some 23- to 24-inch blades in use.

Motors range from 2½ to 3 horsepower, with 4 horsepower models used to run bigger blades. Mowers are empowered by 2-cycle or 4-cycle engines.

The self-propelled walk-behind usually comes with cutting widths of 21 or 22 inches. Four- and 2-cycle engines are standard in the 3, 3½, and 4 horsepower range.

AMF Western Tool Div.

Power mower with reel blades will give velvety smooth cut on flat and even lawn. Reel mower works better than rotary on formal or semiformal lawn design.

Toro Mfg. Corp.

Hand-pushed mower powered by gasoline engine is the most practical type for the average homeowner. Bag attachment catches cut grass for transport to compost heap.

Like most riding mowers, this 5 hp unit has gasoline-powered engine supplying locomotion in rear of mower. Blade on this model gives 26-inch cutting width.

Allis-Chalmers Corp.

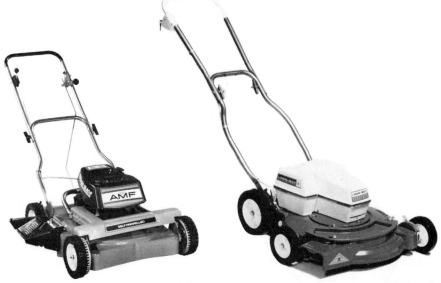

AMF Western Tool Div.

Self-propelled gas-operated mower pulls itself along grass and need only be guided by the operator. It's ideal for large lawns.

Lawn-Boy/OMC Lincoln

Battery-powered electric mower runs on rechargeable packs which can be plugged into household current after mowing. Model cuts a swathe 19 inches wide.

To make it easier to use electric rider mower, some units run on power kept in storage battery. Batteries can be recharged by plugging into house current.

Deere & Company

Most power mowers have gasoline engines for propulsion. However, there are actually three kinds of power mowers made: gasoline-engine mowers, AC electric current mowers, DC battery-operated mowers.

By far the most common type of power engine is the gasoline engine, an adaptation of the outboard motor developed for boats.

You start the power-mower engine by pulling a rope. You stop it by grounding out the engine with a switch that simply cuts out the spark.

Some lawn mowers are powered by house current—60 cycle AC at 120 volts—and these can be recognized by the cord that runs from the mower to the house. The advantage of this type of mower is that you do not need to pull a rope to start it.

There are drawbacks, however, because of the presence of the electric cord. In mowing with an electric cord attached to the mower, you must run parallel to the house, keeping the cord always out of the wheels.

In order to avoid the constant threat of cutting the cord, some manufacturers have built electric-powered machines which utilize DC electric current supplied by batteries. In some models, the battery is in the mower itself. Others supply power packs that the operator wears as he pushes the mower along.

SAFETY WITH POWER MOWERS. A power mower must be considered a dangerous machine. You must observe safety measures not only as you mow, but before you start.

Before mowing with a power mower, you should:

- Read the operator's manual *very* carefully. Understand every word before you touch the machine.
- Learn how to stop the engine quickly in case of emergency.
- Make sure the lawn is clear of sticks, stones, wire, and debris.
- Clear the area of all children and pets.
- Fill the gas tank.
- Wear proper clothing: no shorts, sandals, or bare feet.
- Start the mower carefully, standing with your feet well away from the blades.
- Do not operate the engine where carbon monoxide fumes might collect.

Jacobsen Mfg. Co.

With walking mower, push machine across the face of slope laterally. With riding mower, however, mow up and down slope vertically.

With electric mower powered by household current, mow back and forth across lawn as shown to avoid cutting the cord. Two electric convenience outlets make mowing easier. Start at house and work halfway across lawn. Then plug in at far end and work back to middle.

During mowing, you should:
- Keep your hands, feet, sticks, and everything but grass from the mower housing.
- Do not unclog the mower discharge while the mower is running.
- Always push the machine ahead of you; do not pull it toward you.
- With a walking mower, mow a slope across the face laterally.
- With a riding mower, mow up and down a slope, vertically.
- Watch out for holes and hidden hazards in the turf.
- With a riding mower, look behind you while backing up.
- Keep your feet away from the discharge side.
- Do not direct the discharge chute toward bystanders.
- Stop the engine each time you leave the machine.
- Disengage the mowing mechanism before crossing drives, walks, or roads.
- Do not leave the starter in a cocked position.
- In an AC electric mower, keep the cord out of the mower's path.
- Do not use an AC electric mower when the grass is wet. Do not operate in the rain. Make sure the mower is always well grounded.
- Store an electric mower well out of range of children and power outlets where it might be plugged in.

When servicing the mower, you should:
- Be sure the shields and safety devices are in place before turning on the motor.
- Always turn off the engine before cleaning. Then disconnect the spark plug wire so the blade cannot be turned by the engine.
- Do not overspeed the engine or alter the governor settings at any time. Excessive speed is dangerous and shortens the machine's life.

WATERING YOUR LAWN. By weight and composition, a grass plant is usually about 85 per cent water. Almost 95 per cent of the daily absorption of water from the soil is transpired into the air through the grass blade. Grass can stay green and vigorous only if its roots are directly in contact with fresh water.

Almost any lawn will suffer sometime during the summer months from lack of water, for few communities get enough rain throughout all the summer months. You should water a lawn about once a week.

Your lawn will need about an inch of water a week to keep it green throughout the summer. In a dry climate, you have to run a typical lawn sprinkler a couple of hours or more in one spot to give the grass this much water. A steady all-day rain may not even add up to an inch of water.

You should anticipate a need for sprinkling *before* your grass goes brown to prove it.

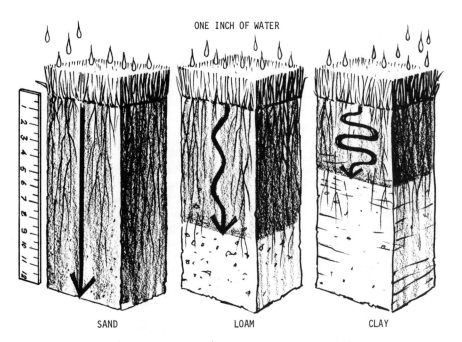

ONE INCH OF WATER

SAND   LOAM   CLAY

In ordinary dry soil, one inch of water will penetrate sandy soil about 12 inches deep because of porous quality of sand. It will sink 6 to 10 inches in loam, which is mixture of dirt, sand and clay. In clay, it will only penetrate 4 to 5 inches. Because sandy soil drains so quickly, both loam- and sand-supported lawns require more frequent watering than clay-supported lawns.

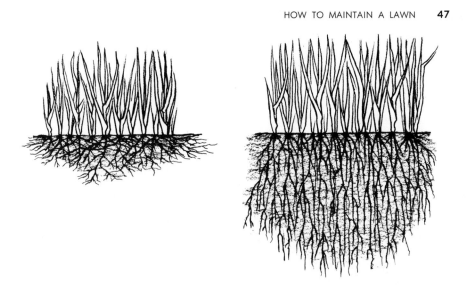

Daily light watering of grass (left) produces shallow roots that die in summer's heat. Weekly deep watering (right) creates strong, enduring roots.

You can find out whether or not your grass needs water by cutting into the soil a couple of inches. Pull out a sample plug. Test the soil. If the dirt feels moist when rubbed between your fingers, you don't need to water the lawn.

If it's at all dry, you do need to water. Don't forget, soil dries out quickly, and when it has no more water in it, the grass roots have nowhere else to go to get it.

To find out exactly how much water your sprinkler delivers, set out several flat-bottomed tin cans at various positions on your lawn. Turn on your sprinkler and let it run for an hour. Then measure the depth of water in each of the cans with a ruler. You can figure out how many hours during the week you will have to run the sprinkler to supply the lawn with an inch of water.

If a part of your lawn wilts quickly at the first onset of high temperatures, the grass may have shallow roots. Try pulling up the turf. If it comes up easily and separates from the sod, it is quite likely that the grass suffers from roots that are too short.

Shallow roots are caused by waterlogging—too much water in the fall and spring. The roots cannot go down deeper because they will not grow through the water that is trapped there, and they do not grow long enough. Because they are short, the slightest bit of heat and sun will make the blades above ground wilt.

You can solve the problem of shallow roots by giving the area where heat wilt is evident frequent waterings. Keeping the surface of the ground moist allows the plants to push their roots down into solid soil.

During hot summer weather, insect activity may severely damage areas of the lawn. It is quite a common mistake to assume that this damage is due to a lack of moisture. Obviously, watering the lawn will not cure pest damage. However, watering every day may help the grass to fight any invading enemy. Watering will also help the fading out of certain grasses, or the browning of matted patches of grass.

WATERING PROBLEMS. If your lawn does not respond to mowing and watering, the following problems may be responsible.

Faulty sprinkler set-up. Your water sprinkler may continually miss certain lawn areas around the perimeter, or under bushes that shed water. Or the wind may blow the water away from certain parts. Study your sprinkler system and analyze the reason certain areas are not watered sufficiently.

New seedings. If you have put down new seeds and want to nourish them, you must keep the surface soil constantly wet until the grass is moist and well-rooted. On warm, dry days you may have to water in the mid-morning, noontime, and late afternoon.

Tree-shaded areas. Soil will stay moist longer in areas that are shaded from the sun. However, in the late summer and early fall the grass under tall trees may be the first to need water. The tree roots exert a greater demand on the moisture as leaf-fall time approaches, and the roots rob the soil of the water that would otherwise go to the grass roots. To remedy this situation, just give those areas more water if you notice browning.

Garden and lawn aids include impulse and ball-turret sprinklers on spike stands; adjustable-flow soaker for plants, trees and shrubs; two-way and single-hose shut-offs; adjustable hose nozzle; and fan spray.

Plasmet Engr. Corp.

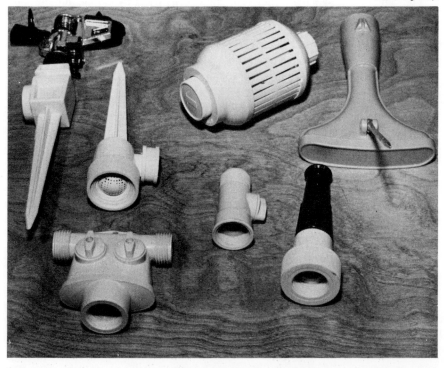

WATERING NOTES.

- Lawn grasses need the equivalent of about 1 inch of water a week through the summer months.
- Water your lawn so that it receives about ½ inch every 3 days.
- Lawns need more water in hot, windy periods of high evaporation when the soil dries faster. Slopes facing the south or the west also need more water.
- Water any time of the day you find convenient—morning, noon, or night.
- In the late spring, your lawn may need watering about one week before the onset of the hot spell.
- In a typical May-through-September season, rainfall will probably take care of half your lawn's needs. But you must supply the rest, or the grass will turn brown.

SPRINKLING SYSTEMS. There are many kinds of portable sprinkler systems now available that can make your lawn-watering problems more bearable than the old-fashioned hand-held hose.

Spike sprinkler. A simple spray attachment mounted on a spike that is speared into the grass in the center of the area to be watered.

Three lawn sprinklers include impulse, two-arm, and ball turret—with controlled-circle impulse sprinkler at left adjustable as to direction and area to be covered and as to distance and height of throw. Middle unit is circular sprinkler. Dial-a-Spray unit at right waters in three patterns—10 by 50 feet, 20 by 40 feet, and 30 by 30 feet.

Plasmet Engr. Corp.

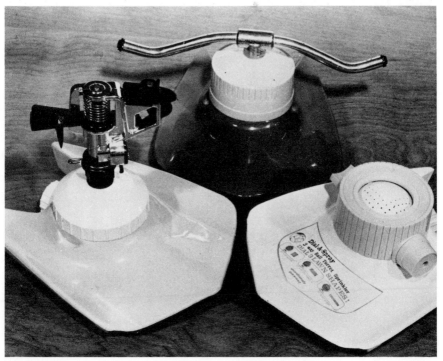

L. R. Nelson Mfg. Co. Inc.

Portable sprinkling unit sends water out in circle as it slowly traverses lawn. Throw will encompass entire strip during one traverse.

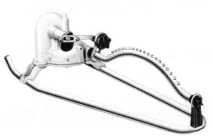

L. R. Nelson Mfg. Co. Inc.

Oscillating sprinkler can be set to water full or partial lawn areas. Sprinkler works by water pressure operating on a permanently sealed mechanism.

Melnor

Traveling sprinkler walks along hose as it slowly unreels from portable unit. While sprinkler travels, it sprays water in a circle over top of hose.

Circular sprayer. A portable unit designed to throw water in a uniform circle radiating from a particular spot.

Impulse sprinkler. A newer development that features adjustable controls covering a 20- to 40-foot radius, part-circle settings, back-splash protection, and a stable base that will not crawl.

Oscillating sprinkler. Features finger-tip control for watering full or partial areas, covering up to 2,800 square feet, with a permanently sealed motor.

Although any of these small portable sprinklers is adequate, it is much easier to have an automatic sprinkler system installed in the lawn itself—particularly one that can be controlled from turn-on valve installations.

Actually, any healthy, well-tended lawn deserves a sprinkler system of its own to insure the right amount of water at the right place at the right time.

PLANNING A SPRINKLER SYSTEM. The most important step in the installation of a sprinkling system is the planning. First of all, make a detailed plan of your grounds, house, and property lines on graph paper calibrated in squares $1/10$ inch wide. Draw in all these features:

Property lines	Garden areas	High areas
House	Plants and shrubs	Low areas
Garage	Trees	Outdoor lights
Water meter hookup	Paved areas	Mail box
Sewer lines	Walls	Planters
Lawn areas	Direction of wind	Any other constructions

Semipermanent sprinkler waters area as large as 2,500 square feet, or can be adjusted to cover rectangular shapes. Thin line in foreground of photo marks 4-inch-deep slit where a flexible pipe joins the sprinkler to outside faucet.

Toro Mfg. Corp.

Any automatic sprinkler system is composed of several main parts:

Sprinkler main valve (one or more)

Sprinkler heads

Connecting pipes (underground)

The sprinkler main valve is a turn-on valve located in an accessible spot not covered by spray from the sprinkler heads it controls.

The sprinkler heads are of two kinds, one modeled for lawn use, the other modeled for shrubbery use.

The lawn type is called a pop-up sprinkler head. It is mounted flush with the lawn, and pops up under water pressure to deliver its spray.

The shrubbery type is mounted above the ground so that the spray will be thrown higher onto shrubs and plants.

Both pop-up and shrubbery heads come in full circle, half-circle, and quarter-circle spray patterns. Each sprinkler head is designed to discharge a specific number of gallons of water per minute — *gpm* — over a given radius and each head requires a certain degree of water pressure per square inch — *psi* — to accomplish its job.

Find out what static water pressure is delivered to your house. Then consult the chart of Maximum Gallons per Minute to find out exactly how many your *psi* will deliver.

With a *psi* of 60, a ¾ valve main using ½ PVC pipe will supply 14 *gpm* to one sprinkler head.

Because of the variations in water pressure not only from street to street but from summer to winter and from a.m. to p.m., be sure to find out all about expected *psi* fluctuations before continuing your plan.

For every specific *psi* delivered you can get a proper sprinkler valve and head, but each must be to the exact specifications.

Sprinkler mains. Your lot plan may call for more than one sprinkler main. Most homes need at least two — one in front, the other in back. Once you have determined the locations of each main valve, you can arrange the heads around each main.

Incidentally, sprinkler valves are unsightly if they are located in the middle of a natural lawn or garden. Try to conceal them if possible — under a shrub, behind a rock, back of a hedge. Don't forget to put the valves where you can operate them without wetting yourself.

MAXIMUM GALLONS PER MINUTE (GPM) ALLOWABLE FOR EACH SPRINKLER

VALVE GROUPING

Length of Supply lines	Sizes of:				Static water pressure (psi)					
	Water meter	Supply lines	Sprinkler		30	40	50	60	70	80
			Valve	PVC Pipe	Gallons per minute (gpm)					
50 ft. max.	¾″	¾″	¾″	½″	6	9	12	14	16	18
	¾″	1″	1″	¾″	10	13	17	19	23	26
100 ft. max.	¾″	¾″	¾″	½″	5	7	9	12	13	15
	¾″	1″	1″	¾″	7	12	15	18	20	23

NOTE: Supply lines should include applicable length of service line and sprinkler main.

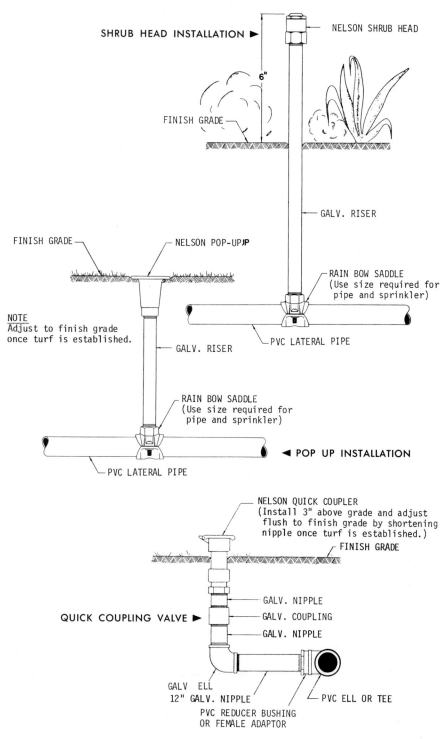

SHRUB HEAD INSTALLATION ▶

NELSON SHRUB HEAD

6"

FINISH GRADE

GALV. RISER

RAIN BOW SADDLE
(Use size required for
pipe and sprinkler)

FINISH GRADE

NELSON POP-UP**JP**

NOTE
Adjust to finish grade
once turf is established.

GALV. RISER

PVC LATERAL PIPE

RAIN BOW SADDLE
(Use size required for
pipe and sprinkler)

◀ POP UP INSTALLATION

PVC LATERAL PIPE

NELSON QUICK COUPLER
(Install 3" above grade and adjust
flush to finish grade by shortening
nipple once turf is established.)

FINISH GRADE

GALV. NIPPLE

GALV. COUPLING

QUICK COUPLING VALVE ▶

GALV. NIPPLE

GALV ELL
12" GALV. NIPPLE

PVC ELL OR TEE

PVC REDUCER BUSHING
OR FEMALE ADAPTOR

Coverage. Once you have decided where the sprinkler main valves will be, study the lot plan. With a compass, draw circles around positions where you think you want sprinkler heads, showing exactly what area each head will cover.

If you've decided to go along with standard heads, each covering a 24-foot-diameter circle, set your compass to a 1.2-inch radius and draw a circle around each head. This will give you an idea of the coverage.

Start in with the corners of the lawn areas, using quarter-circle heads, then move to the lateral borders and put in half-circle heads, and finally go to the center of the area and put in the full-circle head.

All circles, half circles, and quarter circles should overlap at least once, leaving no place on the lawn uncovered.

For maximum coverage, follow these rules:

● Always overlap the outer third of a spray radius.

● Design your system so that water is always thrown from the perimeter of the lawn toward the center.

● Be sure every spot on the lawn or garden is covered by at least one spray head.

● Plan separate lawn and garden sprinkling systems. Water the lawns with one system; water the gardens and shrubs with another system. The two do not mix well, for each system requires a special type of head and serves a specific purpose.

GPM requirements. Now comes some tough figuring. In order to find out the size of valves required to operate each sprinkler main, you will have to know the gallon per minute requirements for each sprinkler head, *and* the total gallonage required by the system.

To do this, first determine the total number of gallons your input will produce; then determine how many valves you can accommodate. Group the sprinkler heads together, making certain that the allowable amount of water is not exceeded.

INSTALLING THE SYSTEM. The first step is to assemble the valve system:

● Put together the valve assembly for the sprinkler main valve with PVC (plastic) adaptors.

● Cut in the tee joint fitting for the sprinkler main.

● Dig trenches to each of the valves.

● Lay the pipe connecting the valves.

● Install the valves and flush them out.

● Check the system for leaks.

Next, stake the entire layout. Use string and stakes to mark the location of each of the sprinkler heads.

Now dig the trenches for the sprinkler head connections. Use a flat-edged spade and dig V-shaped trenches about 5 inches wide at the top and about 6 to 8 inches deep.

The next step is to assemble the plastic piping that connects the heads to the sprinkler mains. With a hacksaw, cut the PVC pipe to length. Weld the PVC pipe and fittings together by applying a thin coat of PVC solvent to the inside of the fitting and the outside of the pipe. Wait 12 hours, then insert plastic risers, using PVC tees cut into the PVC piping. Flush out the pipelines and install the sprinkler heads to the risers.

Now test the system for proper lawn coverage. Turn on each valve and let the water flow. Check the heads for accuracy to see that the area is properly covered. Lower the pop-up heads to the proper level.

Finally, backfill the trenches, filling each trench a little higher than the bottom of the sod surrounding it and tamping to the proper level.

FERTILIZING A LAWN. The third important point in lawn maintenance – after proper mowing and watering – is the proper application of fertilizer.

It is a rare soil that contains enough of the natural chemicals necessary to keep a turf green and strong. Many home lawns exist in a perpetual state of starvation and exhaustion. The effective fertilizing of an established lawn includes at least three annual applications of plant food, timed for early spring, mid-spring, and late summer.

Complete fertilizers. The kinds of fertilizers you use on an established lawn are either "complete" fertilizers, or simply nitrogenous materials.

A complete fertilizer contains three elements: nitrogen, phosphoric acid, and potash, each required by plants and obtained by them from the soil. Fertilizer preparations are labeled according to the amount of these three elements.

For instance, a bag of 8-6-4 mix contains 8 pounds of nitrogen (N), 6 pounds of phosphoric acid (P), and 4 pounds of potash (K). That equals a total of 18 pounds of these elements. The remainder of the 100 pounds – 82 – is made up of the balance of the compounds that supply these three elements to the mix.

Nitrogen, phosphoric acid, and potash are not the *only* elements required by a soil. Soil also needs calcium, magnesium, sulphur, iron, and traces of copper, manganese, zinc, and boron. Lime compounds usually supply enough calcium and magnesium to suit the average lawn. The rest of these elements are usually present in most soils in sufficient quantities, or are added as parts of the impurities in the compounds that furnish in a complete fertilizer the amounts of N, P, and K. You can disregard consideration of these secondary elements.

Many different ratios of complete fertilizers are on the market. Since nitrogen is the most important element needed by grass, most of the ratios show more N than P or K: 10-6-4, or 8-6-2 give good results for most lawns.

However, all ratios vary according to soil conditions, and other ratios can give as good results. One prepared especially for a specific lawn after a soil test is the best mix possible.

If there are no directions for lawn use on the bag you buy, you can get an idea of the amount of fertilizer to use by studying the nitrogen content.

Spring. For early spring use, take the first number in the formula, divide 100 by it, and apply this number of pounds per 1,000 square feet. With an 8-6-2, divide 100 by 8 for 12½; use 12½ pounds per 1,000 square feet. With a 10-6-4, divide 100 by 10 for 10, and use 10 pounds per 1,000 square feet. These amounts will provide 1 pound of nitrogen for every 1,000 square feet, ⅛ and 1/10 respectively of the total 100 pounds in each mix.

Mid-spring. Use the same amount of fertilizer in your second application near mid-spring.

Late summer. Double the key number for use in September or late summer. For 8-6-2, use 12½ times 2, or 25 pounds per 1,000 square feet; for 10-6-4, use 10 times 2 or 20 pounds per 1,000 square feet. You can see that this formula will provide you with a total of 4 pounds of nitrogen per 1,000 square feet throughout the summer (1, 1, and 2 equals 4).

Nitrogen. Nitrogen in fertilizer may be derived from either organic or inorganic compounds. Organic compounds may be either natural or synthetic.

For lawn maintenance, at least half of the nitrogen provided should come from organic sources. You must specify this when you buy fertilizer. Organic nitrogen lasts for several weeks in the soil. Inorganic nitrogen gives immediate results, but its effectiveness lasts for only several days.

Some experts insist that organic nitrogen should be derived from natural organic rather than synthetics for treatment of turf grass. However, there is no real proof that natural organic nitrogen is superior to synthetic nitrogen at the present time.

Fertilizer manufacturers get natural organic nitrogen from such sources as castor pomace, cottonseed meal, activated sewage sludge, tankage, and blood meal.

Many homeowners have found that the use of this element alone will maintain a good lawn. Nitrogenous materials from organic sources, of course, have some small quantities of phosphoric acid and potash in them as well.

Perhaps you may be able to fertilize with natural organic nitrogen alone, but you would be wise to use a complete fertilizer (all three elements) at least once, preferably in the first application of the year.

If you are using castor pomace, cottonseed meal, and activated sewage, apply them at the rate of 20 to 25 pounds per 1,000 square feet for the first and second applications, and 40 to 50 pounds for the last. Do not inhale the dust from castor pomace—it is very poisonous.

Fertilizer applicators. You can use a simple spreader—the same kind you use to seed a lawn—when you apply an organic fertilizer. Be sure that you apply it evenly. If you overlap certain parts, they will remain yellow and burn the grass. The best kind of spreader to use is one calibrated to dispense exact amounts of the fertilizer constant throughout the lawn area.

After applying fertilizer to a lawn, water it in by sprinkling the entire area. Do not flood the lawn, or the fertilizer will be washed away or strung out along depressions and sags in the lawn; the concentration there will cause burns. Water evenly and gently.

If you use a *natural* organic, you do not need to water it in. Natural fertilizers do not burn grass.

Do not use a complete fertilizer on a new lawn until at least two months after germination. Otherwise, you will kill the young grass.

Liquid fertilizer. The newest addition to the fertilizer arsenal is "liquid" fertilizer. It is easier to apply than solid fertilizer, because you can use a sprayer, a watering can, or a suction device attached to the hose. Nor will liquid fertilizer burn grass.

Most liquid fertilizers contain the same complete formula regular fertilizers contain—N, P, K, and sometimes other elements. You can learn about the contents of each from the containers. Complete directions are always provided. Follow them.

Liquid fertilizers do not last long in the soil. Smaller amounts of N, P, and K are provided, too; you will have to repeat applications of liquid fertilizer more often than solid fertilizer. The directions on each mix will give you the proper timing for regular applications.

Even though most liquid fertilizers cost more per pound, they are much easier to use and will give you excellent results.

Lime. The use of lime is very tricky, because not all soils need it. However, all lawns *do* use lime and will deteriorate if they do not get it. Lime is a soil sweetener that also tends to overcome excess acidity.

Lime serves to make the elements in the fertilizer more available to the grass plants. It also tends to cut down the possibility that poisonous elements will injure the plants. And it helps promote the proper granulated soil structure that in turn gives a deep-rooted, drought-resistant turf.

Lime is not considered an actual fertilizer; it simply prepares the soil for better utilization of fertilizer elements.

Test your soil first to see if you need lime. If you do, apply it some time in the late autumn. This allows the lime to work down into the soil through the winter months.

If you apply weed killers, insecticides, and complete fertilizers, do not apply lime at the same time or very soon after. Wait a week or two. However, you can apply lime with a complete fertilizer *before* seeding.

You do not need to water in limes that are not caustic. Most forms of lime can be applied with a fertilizer spreader. However, some of them are so finely ground that you have to spread them by hand. Do not let lime pile up on the turf, or it will cake up when moisture settles in.

For lawn turf, use lime in the forms of ground limestone, dolomitic limestone, hydrated lime, or ground oyster shells. Hydrated lime is also known as mason's hydrate, water-slaked lime, or agricultural lime.

Do not use caustic lime for turf. Caustic lime is also called builder's lime, quick lime, burnt lime or lump lime. You'll burn your lawn with it—and probably your hands as well.

Sulfur. If a soil test shows that the pH of your soil is too high—that is, that it is too alkaline—apply sulfur to make it more acid. Before rushing in with the sulfur, however, ask the soil analyst the exact amount to use and find out the best way to apply it.

Gypsum. In some cases, your soil pH may require some calcium. You can provide calcium by applications of gypsum. Many golf course caretakers use gypsum to cut down on subsoil compaction on the green and fairways where there are lumps far below a level that can be reached by aerating tools.

P. D. Stout Co.

Designed to aerate and loosen compacted turf and soil, shoes of plastic and steel penetrate earth 1½ inches below the sole. Holes allow air and water to reach roots of grass.

Simplicity Mfg. Co. Inc.

Attachment for lawn revitalization performs four vital lawn-care functions by raising thatch to the top of the lawn, aerating soil without compacting it, pruning roots so healthy grass plants have room to grow, and building miniature irrigation system to permit water and fertilizer penetration to grass roots. Unit fits most riding mowers.

Apply gypsum sometime in mid-autumn, at about 50 to 75 pounds per 1,000 square feet. The calcium will work on the soil compaction over the winter months.

AERATING A LAWN. Even with the best kind of cultivation and turning of the soil ahead of time, the average turf may eventually become clogged underneath — compacted is the term used by turf experts — prohibiting air, water, and fertilizer from reaching the grass roots. Aeration is the term used for loosening up this soil to enable needed nourishment to reach the grass roots.

Compacted areas show up in turfs after many people have walked across them, or after the ground itself has tightened up beneath the surface. You should aerate these areas at least once every two months.

You can aerate soil by hand, or you can rent or buy expensive power-driven equipment that will do the job swiftly and painlessly.

Aerate in any month of the growing season. You may kill the turf if you aerate on a hot day without watering the lawn immediately afterward. Continue to irrigate the lawn each day until the holes made by the aerating equipment close over.

Aerating equipment. There are two kinds of aerating equipment: the spiker and the corer. The spiker consists of a small spike disc that penetrates the soil to a depth of about an inch. The spiker makes many small holes in the dirt, breaking up the compacted surface crust. You can use a spiker also to make a seedbed on established turf just before reseeding. In many ways a spiker resembles a tiller.

The corer is a large power-driven machine that takes out large cores of soil 4 to 5 inches deep.

There are also machines that are combinations of these two basic types.

DETHATCHING. The terms used for debris that clusters around each blade of grass at ground level is "thatch." Dead cuttings, broken leaves, and other debris mats up into a compact thatch – like an old-fashioned English cottage roof – preventing water and air from entering into the topsoil.

Thatch can strangle new grass and kill old grass. By collecting all grass clippings when you mow, you can prevent thatch from collecting; however, clippings give back a great deal of nourishment to the soil. It is best to let the clippings lie there, and dethatch the dead material when necessary.

Certain power aerators have dethatching equipment that loosens the thatch around the grass and scoops it up from the soil. If you do not have access to dethatching equipment, rake the area carefully with a flexible garden rake, and water carefully to float out all loosened debris. Then rake again to get out all the remaining thatch.

TOPDRESSING. Spreading a layer of loam or humus over the surface of a lawn in order to enrich lawn growth is called "topdressing." Although topdressing is not a real necessity, it does accomplish a few things that nothing else can:

- It prepares a lawn for re-seeding.
- It forms a type of mulch on dry slopes.
- It helps to fill depressions.

The loam applied in topdressing is usually spread on at a rate of $\frac{1}{2}$ cubic yard per 1,000 square feet. After carefully distributing it over the surface of the lawn, work it into the grass with the back of the rake, or brush it in by dragging a plank over the lawn.

Use a good sandy loam topsoil, or if topsoil is in short supply, use a mixture of $\frac{1}{3}$ humus and $\frac{2}{3}$ topsoil. Humus materials that can be used to enrich the soil can be rotted manure, compost, cultivated peat moss, or used-up mushroom soil.

OVERSEEDING. One way to spruce up an old lawn and make it come up greener in the spring is to spread a quantity of ryegrass seed onto the existing turf in the late fall, anytime from October to December. This procedure, called "overseeding," will work only with cool-season grasses. Here are the proper steps to take in an overseeding program:

(1) Prepare the lawn surface by aerating and dethatching in the usual fashion. Aeration will open up the soil and dethatching will break up masses of material to let the new grass grow through.

(2) Attach a pick-up bag to your lawn mower. Set the mower to half its normal cutting height. Mow the lawn in two directions, at right angles to each other, to be sure to pick up all the clippings of the cut grass and all the dead material from the dethatching.

(3) Seed the lawn, spreading ryegrass either by hand or by spreader.

(4) Water the lawn carefully to wash the seeds down into the soil. Keep the turf moist, but do not flood it.

(5) You can either roll the lawn lightly, to press the seeds down into the soil, or topdress the lawn.

(6) Be sure to *keep the lawn moist* until the new grass comes up! This is the most important step in overseeding; the ground must be kept moist to encourage the new grass to grow and to permit it to come up easily.

Ryegrass is the best variety to use for overseeding. It is inexpensive, plentiful, and it germinates quickly in three to seven days. Ryegrass, incidentally, is susceptible to diseases like dollar spot, rust and damping-off.

Jacobsen Mfg. Co.

Keep all paths and areaways wide enough for easy passage of mowing equipment.

Avoid slopes that are impossible to mow by planting them with ground cover rather than grass.

Keep grass away from flower beds and provide brick mowing edge for shrubs, foundation plants and flowers.

Circular bed of bricks protects tree from equipment and makes for neater yard.

Put brick mowing edge around utility pipes and other surface obstructions to eliminate trimming and edging problems.

Use brick border next to house, eliminating unsightly weeds and the need for close mowing and trimming.

Other cool-season grasses can be used to overseed, but they take longer to germinate than ryegrass. As an alternate to ryegrass you can use a mixture of *Poa trivialis,* red fescue, and Kentucky bluegrass.

Overseeding is not recommended for warm-season lawns, because Bermuda grass and zoysia turfs – and most of the grasses that respond well to hot weather – grow too densely. This density prevents other leaves from coming up through the tightly knit turf.

LAWN MAINTENANCE PROGRAM. Assuming that your lawn has become well-established, you should prepare a step-by-step program through the year that will keep it maintained. Regular care is the secret of a great lawn.

Here is a skeleton list to remind you:

Spring

(1) Roll the lawn lightly. Freezing and thawing through the winter months sometimes heaves up the turf and breaks it. If the lawn is not rolled, the exposed soil might dry out. Use a roller only heavy enough to press the turf lightly back in place.

(2) Renovate areas in the lawn that have become thin or sparse. Loosen the soil to a depth of about 2 or 3 inches, working in an area 3 or 4 feet in diameter. Add in organic material like peat moss or humus, and superphosphate. Work in these materials, level the area and scratch it lightly.

(3) Seed the renovated areas with a permanent lawn mix of fescue and bluegrass.

(4) Roll the renovated areas to keep the seed firmly in place. Water the seeded area.

(5) About the first half of April, apply the first lawn feeding. Use a high nitrogen, slow-release lawn fertilizer. Spread it with a spreader, applying 10 to 20 pounds per 1,000 square feet. If you want a good growth, apply a second feeding about three or four weeks later.

(6) Lime the soil if it is acid, sandy, or if it needs lime according to soil tests. Do not overlime, or you will encourage the growth of clover and weeds.

(7) Compacted areas in the lawn discourage grass growth. Aerate the soil early in the spring.

(8) Spread peat moss, leaf mold, or compost in a thin layer over the aerated turf. Rake it in gently. This layer will hold in moisture and warmth.

(9) When the temperature gets up to about 50 degrees, apply herbicides to wipe out dandelions and plantains.

(10) Seed again to fill in the areas made bare by weed controllers.

(11) Crabgrass is coming! Exert pre-emergent controls early in April.

(12) Start mowing as soon as the lawn is established. Early on, let it grow 2 or 2½ inches high. Mow high and frequently, never cutting off more than one quarter of the blade. Keep your mower sharp. Alternate mowing patterns: north-south once, east-west once, northeast-southwest once, and so on.

Summer Care

(1) Cut the grass at a slower rate in July and August than you did in the spring. Cut the lawn no closer than 1¼ inches to 1½ inches on warm, dry days. Keep it at 2 inches in the heat of summer.

(2) Watering is important during the dry, hot days of summer. Bentgrass lawns need more water; fescues need little and are drought-resistant; blue-grasses require some water. Light, sandy soils need more water than clay soils. Do not water

frequently and lightly, but infrequently and heavily. Soak the soil to a 6-inch depth. Water before the grass starts to wilt.

(3) Attack crabgrass and pests in the summer months. Fungus growth is at a minimum in the hot days, so skip that. If you still have crabgrass, use a post-emergent chemical treatment.

(4) Chinch bugs appear during the summer months. Dust for them, using three to five dustings a season, starting in June and working through September.

Fall Care

(1) Repeat the feeding again before winter comes.

(2) Seed in the thin spots to prepare for spring.

(3) Use herbicides — 2,4-D, or 2,4,5-T.

(4) Remove thatch from the lawn in early fall.

(5) Check the pH of your soil again to determine its acid-alkaline balance. Hit for 6 to 6.5. Below 5, you'll need lime. If you re-seed, add lime anyway.

(6) Feed the grass with a complete fertilizer for the third time.

(7) Water the lawn to leach the feeding material down into the roots.

(8) Re-seed at this time. Apply seed with a spreader, and then saturate the area with a thin spray of water. Keep the soil moist until green begins to show.

4 | Keeping Your Lawn Healthy

IN SPITE OF ALL THE HARD LABOR and care you have lavished on it, your lawn turf may begin to deteriorate — and for a number of very different reasons.

Here are the four principal causes of turf trouble:

(1) Physical and chemical deficiencies in the soil.
(2) Fungus diseases.
(3) Pests.
(4) Attack by weeds.

Although a lawn grass attacked by a fungus disease, by pests, or made weak by soil deficiencies might appear in several cases to be suffering exactly the same ailment, the cause for each sickness may be different and the method of curing it different too.

Many adverse conditions can affect a lawn because of soil deficiencies, each manifesting itself in a special way. Each condition can be cured in a particular way.

In the following section, some of these adverse conditions are described, along with their causes and cures.

SOIL DEFICIENCY

CONDITION: The turf grows thin and weedy in an irregular circle, but as the weather turns hot, the grass in the circular patch dies out.

CAUSE: There is a stone and/or stones under the surface of the turf.

CURE: Probe for the stone and/or stones, remove it/them, fill the hole with topsoil, fertilize, and re-seed the patch.

CONDITION: Same as above.

CAUSE: Layers of peat moss or sand have become lodged an inch or so below the turf, cutting off nourishment.

CURE: Cut out a plug of soil about 2 inches deep and examine it. Dig up the grass over the patch, mix topsoil in with the peat moss or sand, then fertilize and re-seed the patch.

CONDITION: The turf grows thin and full of weeds in certain sections, and then, as the weather turns hot and dry, the grass becomes blue and wilts.

CAUSE: There is not enough topsoil in all parts of the lawn.

CURE: Turn over the poor parts with a pitchfork, add additional topsoil, fertilize and re-seed.

CONDITION: Although the lawn is mowed at correct height and is adequately fertilized, traffic causes path lines to appear; plantains and knotweeds thrive.

CAUSE: There is soil compaction underneath the traffic lines.

CURE: Aerate the compacted soil as explained in "Aeration Procedure."

CONDITION: The tips of the grass, especially fescues, turn white and brown after mowing.

CAUSE: The mower is dull or the blades poorly adjusted.
CURE: Adjust the mower and the blades.

CONDITION: There are large or small scorched areas in the turf.
CAUSE: The lawn mower has allowed gasoline, fuel oil, or machine oil to drip onto the turf.
CURE: Water the area heavily, and if the grass does not recover, re-seed the patch. Where fuel oil has been repeatedly splashed, the grass will never be right. Cut out a plug of sod from another section of lawn and plant it.

CONDITION: There are scorched or yellow patches here and there with luxuriant grass on their borders.
CAUSE: Animal urine has burned the grass.
CURE: Same as above. Also, keep dogs off the lawn.

CONDITION: There are burns not caused by gasoline, urine, or fertilizer.
CAUSE: Winter road salts may have been splashed on the lawn from the street.
CURE: Remove the chemical on the lawn by watering, although the thaw will often carry away these salts.

CONDITION: The grass is scorched brown in spreader tracks, or where handfuls of plant food material have been thrown down.
CAUSE: Chemicals and fertilizers have burned the grass.
CURE: Water the burned area heavily, and if the grass does not recover soon, re-seed the patch. Give the grass every chance to come back before replanting.

CONDITION: The grass is sparse and dull green even in periods of good growing weather.
CAUSE: It does not have enough fertilizer.
CURE: Apply a complete fertilizer, as explained in "Fertilizing Procedure."

CONDITION: The turf remains thin and weedy even during a good growing season and with the application of the proper fertilizer.
CAUSE: The grass is clipped too closely.
CURE: Raise the height of the mower blade to $1\frac{1}{2}$ inches or more.

CONDITION: Although the lawn has been carefully tended, the grass does not recover from a short drought, and sourgrass grows thickly.
CAUSE: It does not have enough lime.
CURE: Analyze the soil and add exactly the amount of lime called for.

CONDITION: The grass, particularly if it is a fescue, remains brown in a cool spring.
CAUSE: Spring dormancy.
CURE: The grass will become green once the weather warms up. Add fertilizer during dormancy to make the grass green sooner.

CONDITION: The grass remains brown in the summer, especially on non-watered lawns.
CAUSE: Summer dormancy.
CURE: The lawn will recover when the fall rains come, unless the soil is sandy or gravelly.

CONDITION: Black, green, yellow or white scums appear on bare patches in the turf.

CAUSE: They are algae or scums.

CURE: Fertilize the lawn and re-seed the bare patches; this is a serious problem only when the turf cover is extremely sparse.

FUNGUS DISEASES. The natural color of a blade of properly growing grass is a healthy green. If the blade is any other color, there is something wrong: too little watering, incorrect fertilizing, chemical burns, mower damage, and so on. However, if the grass blade has a purplish-red color, or if there are brown or black spots or lesions along the sheath, it is definitely diseased, usually by an attack of a fungus.

The grass will recover by itself when the weather changes from hot to cool and from wet to dry. High temperatures and humidity bring on rapid fungus growth; dry cool air discourages it.

Fungus is spread by wind, water, and grass clippings. To control fungus disease, use a chemical fungicide that will attack the particular fungus ruining the grass. Apply the fungicide twice, allowing a week between applications.

Before applying a fungicide, be sure that the grass isn't simply suffering from any of the soil deficiencies already described. In order to help you make specific identifications of fungus diseases, here are descriptions of a few of the most common.

FUNGUS DISEASES

NAME	SYMPTOMS	TREATMENT
Fairy ring	Large dry spot; toadstools may appear in ring. In summer and fall, ring of dead grass; in spring a dark green ring.	Water and fertilize properly. Remove thatch several times a year. Punch holes one foot deep, 1 inch apart inside and outside circle. Fill with water every day for week; fill with fresh dirt and seed. Check pH for lime needs.
Powdery mildew	Grass appears sprinkled with flour; Kentucky bluegrass most susceptible; most often in dense shade areas.	Mix Kentucky bluegrass with other stronger grasses. Cut down on shade by pruning trees and shrubs. Pick up all grass clippings.
Leaf spot	Tiny spots or lesions on grass blades; tips appear scorched, reddish hue noticeable after mowing. Common Kentucky bluegrass susceptible.	After rainy period spray Leaf-spot fungicide. Also use twice in early spring, 2 weeks between applications. Cut grass infrequently; cut no shorter than 2 inches.
Rust	Grass has reddish brown, reddish-yellow or orange-yellow appearance.	Fertilize and water; add nitrogen. Pick up grass clippings.
Brown patch	Wilted leaf blades inside irregular brown circle, smoky ring around edge. Attains diameter of 2 feet or more overnight.	Dies out when weather changes from moist to dry; rarely fatal to lawn.
Dollar spot	Brown circular patches about size of silver dollar; in late spring or early autumn. Cobwebby growth on patches in morning dew.	Apply nitrogenous fertilizer; water in carefully.
Snow mold	Spots of white, pink, reddish-white or gray in lawn along fences or shady areas.	Apply Snow-mold fungicide in late fall or early winter. In spring, rake or pole to remove cobwebby growth.
Damping off	Seedlings lose green color and plants collapse.	No control. Caused by excessive seeding and fertilizing.

NAME	SYMPTOMS	TREATMENT
Grubs (Japanese beetle, Oriental garden beetle, Asiatic beetle)	Skunks and birds tear at lawn more than usual; large number of mole tunnels. Turf turns brown; grub 2 to 4 inches in soil—a grayish or bluish—white worm curled in semi-circle.	Use recommended fungicide followed by heavy watering.
White grubs (young of June bug, May bug)	Same as for Grubs.	Same as for ordinary Grubs, but use about 3 times as much pesticide, followed by heavy watering.
Chinch bugs	Brown patches in sunniest spots during hot spell; damaged grass stays anchored to ground if pulled; patches contain tiny insects.	Apply pesticide followed by heavy watering.
Sod webworms	Grass eaten off at ground level; white or brown scars about an inch long and wide. Sod webworm lives below scars; grayish to dark colored.	Use same pesticide as for grubs but half strength; follow with heavy watering.
Ground ants	Red or black ants in different sizes; piling up of heaps of sand and dirt.	Same as for Chinch bugs. Spot treatment—¼ teaspoon pesticide at entrance to each nest followed by watering.
Earthworms	Casts all over lawn.	Do not destroy unless very numerous. Use pesticide at 3 times grub strength, then heavy watering.
Tropical earthworms	Greater number of casts. Worms have minute bristles around body, musky odor and whip around hand when held.	Use grub pesticide at 4 times the strength. Follow with numerous waterings for at least 2 days.

APPLICATION OF PESTICIDES. Several different chemicals are available for the control of grubs and pests. Dusts can be applied with an ordinary garden spreader. Liquid solutions can be sprayed onto the lawn with a sprayer or with a garden hose.

Always follow up dust and spray applications with a heavy but careful watering of the lawn. If you are lucky enough to time the application before a rainfall, you will not need to water.

Insecticides differ in their speed of killing and in the length of time they keep the soil clean of infestation. Check the times and speeds on the package.

When using chemical insecticides, follow all directions posted on the container. Most of them include precautions for the handler. Store all chemicals of this nature where children cannot reach them, and keep children and animals off the lawn until the pest-killer is thoroughly watered in.

If you have a fish pond, be sure the lawn run-off does not accidentally flow into it. Fish will die if the slightest bit of insecticide flows into their water.

BIOLOGICAL CONTROL. One special way to take care of enormous concentrations or infestations of Japanese beetle grubs is to bypass insecticides and use the "milky spore treatment" to kill them off. This treatment gives the grubs a fatal disease, but is harmless to other forms of life.

You can purchase this pesticide under different brand names. Inject it into the lawn at intervals of several feet. It takes a few years to spread over the lawn. Actually, it is used where there are a great number of grubs — so many that the ordinary treatment by regular insecticides would be too costly.

The milky spore treatment is most effective in the warmer areas of the country. In cooler climes it does not always work well.

RECOGNITION AND CONTROL OF WEEDS. Good soil conditions stimulate the growth of grasses, but they also sometimes contribute to the growth of weeds and other objectionable plants.

However, there are practices that contribute to the strengthening of lawn grasses while discouraging weed plants. In order to encourage grass and discourage weeds, remember:

(1) Regular mowing at 1½ inches or higher will give you a good lawn turf that keeps out weeds.

(2) Timely fertilizing, 3 times a year—in the spring, mid-summer, and fall—will help the grass grow and keep weed growth to a minimum.

(3) Prompt seeding of bare and thin patches will promote grass growth and discourage weeds.

(4) Liming if required by soil analysis will promote grass growth and cut down on weeds.

Unfortunately, almost any grass lawn will sprout weeds at one time or another, no matter how many of the above practices you follow. Several other practices help contribute to weed growth. Avoid them if possible:

(1) Cutting grass with a dull or badly adjusted mower blade will aid weed growth by tearing up the grass.

(2) Over-watering of lawn grass will contribute to the growth of weeds, as will too many light daily sprinklings of water.

(3) Compaction of the soil that is not corrected by proper aeration will allow the stronger weed plants to grow where grass plants fail.

(4) Frequent rolling of the turf, particularly if the roller is too heavy and if the rolling bends the grass, will help weeds proliferate.

Once the weeds have grown in, there is only one thing you can do: eradicate them.

Modern chemicals provide spectacular results with no injury to the grass itself. However, even though herbicides get rid of the weeds, they do not get rid of the reason the weeds got a foothold in the first place. Once you rid your lawn of weeds, you will be well-advised to pursue practices of lawn maintenance that discourage weed growth.

The weeds described in the following table are for identification purposes. If you already know what kind of weed infests your lawn, look for its name in the listing and study the best way to eliminate it. If you have only a few weeds you should pull them out individually, taking care to get out as much of the root as possible. If you do not know what kind of weed infests your lawn, look at the accompanying illustrations and refer to the listing by number.

There are endless varieties of lawn weeds, and many are missing from this list. However, the most common ones are included.

RECOGNITION AND CONTROL OF CRABGRASS. The most common lawn weed and the one that causes most anguish to the suburban gardener is crabgrass. It is an annual plant that appears regularly each year; if you have it once, you'll surely have it again.

It first appears as a wide-leaved seedling. Soon it grows three flat leaves, and then becomes a clump of broad gray-green leaves. Branched seed heads appear in the summer, and grow in ever-widening circles of stems and leaves. When the frost comes, the plant turns reddish-brown and dies.

LAWN WEEDS

NAME	DESCRIPTION	CURE
Buckhorn Plantain (*Plantago lanceolata*)	Rosette form; heavy underground system of lateral roots. Indicates soil compaction or low fertility.	2,4-D.
Carpet Weed (*Molluga verticilata*)	Grows in upright form or straight along ground. Indicates general lawn neglect.	2,4-D; sodium arsenite.
Common Chickweed (*Stellaria media*)	Grows flat along ground, forming patches.	Remove patch when ground moist; re-seed. Use sodium arsenite; sulfate of ammonia.
Crabgrass (*Digitaria snaguinalis, Digitaria ischaemun*)	Develops from 2-leaf plant in June to mass of creeping stems a foot or more in late summer. First frost leaves strawberry colored patches.	See special section.
Dandelion (*Taraxacum officinale*)	Rosette form with long taproot.	2,4-D.
Ground Ivy, Gill-Over-the-Ground (*Nepeta hederacea*)	Above ground trailing stems that root at each node. Used as ground cover in rock gardens.	2,4-D.
Knotweed, Doorweed (*Polygonum aviculare*)	Starts as 2-leaf seedling, then long, flat ground plant. Indicates compaction or low fertility.	2,4-D; 2,3,5-TP.
Moneywort, Creeping Charley (*Lysimachia nummularia*)	Long creeping stems that root at nodes. Indicates too much water or poor drainage.	2,4-D.
Mouse-ear, Chickweed (*Cerastium vulgatum*)	Grows flat along ground forming patches.	Sodium arsenite, sulphate of ammonia.
Nutgrass (*Cyperus rotundus*)	Grows from roots bearing small tubers. Thrives in poorly drained areas.	See cures in Crabgrass section.
Plaintain (*Plantago major, Plantago rugelli*)	Rosette form with strong root system. Indicates compacted soil.	2,4,5-TP
Imitation Bluegrass (*Poa annua*)	Imitates real bluegrass; dies in summer heat leaving brown patches.	See cures in Crabgrass section.
Purslane, Pusley (*Portulaca oleracea*)	Fleshy leaves and stems.	Rake lawn before mowing, then mowing will remove. If this fails, use 2,4-D.
Quack Grass (*Agropyron repens*)	Often confused with crabgrass.	Dies a month or two after mowing.
Sheep Sorrel, Sourgrass (*Rumex acetosella*)	Strong underground rhizomes, sour taste to leaves. Indicates lack of lime and low fertility.	Liming and fertilizing may cure; otherwise use 2,4,5-T.
Shepherds Purse (*Capsella Bursapastoris*)	Widely distributed throughout the turf.	Will die out after some months of mowing. No treatment necessary.
Spotted Spurge (*Euphorbia maculata*)	Spreads with taproot system; has poisonous juice in roots, stems and leaves. Indicates low fertility.	2,4, 5-T; 2 or 3 applications sodium arsenite.
Yarrow (*Achillea millefolium*)	Tough rhizomes and feathery leaves. Likes drier weather than grass; often disappears with wet weather.	2,4,5-T.

The best way to kill it is to knock out the seeds before they get a chance to grow. Early April is the time to do this job. Because the crabgrass has not yet appeared, control at this time is called "pre-emergent control."

If, however, the seeds have had a chance to grow, you can still fight the plants with "post-emergent" chemicals designed for use during the spring and summer months. A post-emergent killer can be used any time after the seedlings sprout; it will not injure lawn grasses. You should, however, fight crabgrass before the big plants get a foothold in the turf. Then they are much more difficult to rout out.

Once crabgrass is killed, you must feed the grasses in the turf to cover the bare areas the crabgrass has taken over. Crabgrass seeds live in the soil for years; your best bet is to build up your lawn with feed and seed, to overpower the crabgrass and supplant it.

One application of most of the crabgrass killers will get rid of plants that are less than 2 inches tall. For bigger plants, you must apply the herbicide twice, about four to seven days apart.

If the crabgrass should reach the seeding stage, rake your lawn before each mowing. Use a catcher to capture the seed clippings. Get rid of them. You can also get additional control by using a pre-emergent control killer, applying it in October to kill the dormant growth through the winter; then use it again in April before the new seeds sprout.

Herbicides for crabgrass control. Phenyl mercury acetate (PMA) is a very effective crabgrass killer for pre-emergent stages and early stages of crabgrass growth. PMA is safe to use on bentgrass, but it causes a slight burning of Kentucky bluegrass. Fescues and Merion bluegrass are sensitive likewise to PMA. On other grasses, use two or three applications of PMA, seven to ten days apart.

Alkyl ammonium methyl arsonate (AMA) and disodium methyl arsonate (DSMA) work best during the early stages of crabgrass growth. Repeat the treatments weekly,

Diamond Chemical

Herbicides for control of crabgrass can be applied to lawn through hose-end sprayer just as weeds begin to sprout from seedlings.

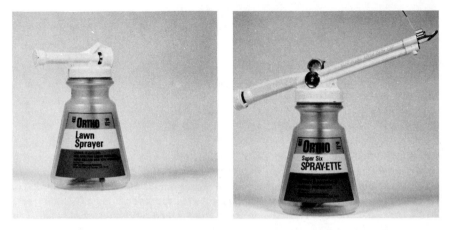

Two types of sprayers can be attached to hose for mixing with water and spraying. Both types work on the principle of water suction.

Crabgrass killer can be applied from aerosol can with pressure of finger. If crabgrass is isolated and can be spotted easily, aerosol application saves use of tank or hose and speeds up operation.

until all the crabgrass disappears. Water the lawn well before each treatment. Bluegrass may be slightly discolored by the treatment, but the discoloration is only temporary. Post-emergent treatment requires twice the application of AMA and DSMA.

Potassium cyanate (KOCN) is a post-emergent control chemical that tends to discolor some grasses, but is excellent for controlling big mature crabgrass coming to seed.

Calcium propyl arsonate (CPA) will help in post-emergent control. It can also be used for pre-emergent control as well.

GENERAL RULES FOR THE USE OF HERBICIDES. The most satisfactory season to use a herbicide is in the spring when the weed's leaves first appear in the lawn. Choose a sunny day for application, a day when no rain is predicted. The herbicide, for effective use, should remain on the plant leaves for several days to do its work. Pick a day when the temperature is over 50 degrees, and when there is no wind. The herbicide should not blow over into plants or into garden areas where it will do great harm. Apply a herbicide about a week or two after the first fertilizing has been accomplished.

Do not spread herbicides over a newly planted lawn; mow for almost a full season before using any herbicide. This chemical will restrict germination of grass seed, and will adversely affect bentgrass even in an established state.

The presence of many different weeds in a lawn indicates that something is wrong with the soil or with your lawn-maintenance practices. The presence of one particular weed indicates that there is a specific condition of the lawn that is helping this weed to thrive. Find out what the condition is, and eliminate it.

5 | Deciduous Trees

IN LANDSCAPING PROPERTY, the tree is the primary planting material at the suburban gardener's command. Each living plant has its proper place in nature; because the tree is the biggest plant of all it must be handled especially carefully in formulating a pleasing picture.

There are two principal reasons for using a planting of any kind: for an artistic or visual effect; or for a practical or utilitarian purpose.

VISUAL EFFECT. If you are planning a landscaping picture for purely visual effect, you should keep in mind the principal elements which count most heavily in the selection of a particular tree—and evaluate each tree in accordance with these considerations:

Beauty. Every tree has its own special beauty. Remember that a tree must blend in with everything else on your lot—house, lawn, shrubs, flowers. If the tree is a spectacular one, the rest of your foliage must be subdued to show it off. If it is graceful, the landscape about it must seem serene. Each tree's beauty must be in balance and harmony with the rest of the scene.

Height. It is obvious that a tree's most important visual impact, aside from its overall configuration, is its vertical height. When selecting a tree, you must always keep in mind its *height at maturity.*

Width. Because the tree is the largest plant alive, its width has a great deal to do with its visual impact. But its width also involves practical considerations. In a crowded suburban lot, a tree that grows too wide can crowd out other plants, can kill them by depriving them of light, air, and food, and can wreck a good artistic concept by overcrowding an area.

Shape. Shape is an important consideration with all deciduous trees, with small trees, with shrubs, with groupings of trees, and most particularly with evergreen trees. The evergreen retains its foliage throughout the year; it will always present the same shape and texture.

Color. Many trees are very showy in their flowering habits. Some have spectacular foliage colors in the fall: green leaves may turn to orange, yellow, and red. Color is a valuable asset to a landscape. It must be used judiciously. Lack of color can be as important as the presence of color, particularly if you are seeking a background for the dramatic display of a brilliant color medley in a garden spot.

Texture. Leaves and branches give a tree its individual texture. The evergreen has a completely different texture from the deciduous; the pine has a different texture from the fir. The evergreen retains its texture, but the deciduous becomes a skeleton in the winter months.

Balance. Because a tree has size and weight, it can act as a balance to another object—either in symmetrical balance or asymmetrical. A group of small trees can be used to balance one large tree; a tall thin tree can be used to balance a short squat

California Redwood Association

Rugged old tree serves as the focal point of this patio garden, its knobby beauty contrasting dramatically with the sleek redwood planks of the adjacent deck.

This Dawyck beech, a columnar form of European beech, offers an arresting silhouette which the suburban gardener can use effectively.

Evergreens like this swirling juniper provide an interesting texture which can be combined with other plants.

Juxtaposition of long-needled pine, left, and thin-leaved honey locust at right, provides an interplay of opposing textures.

one. Because of its size, a tree can be used to balance almost any other kind of planting, grouping, or structure.

Focus. Like people, certain trees grow with character, with dramatic shape, with beauty, with ruggedness, with dependence, with all manner of character traits. A tree that is beautiful, ugly, grotesque, colorful, aged or dwarfed can be used successfully to draw the observer's eye to it. If the tree can stand up to such a viewing, it is worth making the focal point of your yard.

PRACTICAL PURPOSES. If you are planning to use a tree or trees in a landscaping picture for a practical or utilitarian purpose, you should keep in mind the various different uses to which a tree and/or trees can be put:

Specimen. The specimen is a single tree selected and placed in a certain spot in the yard. It stands alone, with no visible support from other trees or groupings. It is best to isolate a specimen, keeping a sharp silhouette so that it can be seen against the skyline. If that is impractical, it should be placed so that it stands out against a wall.

Street trees. In many parts of the country, the street tree is extremely important in beautifying the somber roadways that crisscross our towns. Beautifying a yard is one of the most satisfying experiences of your life. But if the street in front of you does not have proper planting, beautifying it will give you not only pleasure but a sense of helping others.

Background. Trees in groups make excellent backgrounds. A background can line a fence, hide a wall, stand behind a display of brilliant-colored flowers, or even line the end of a spectacular natural lawn terrace. Certain trees serve well as various types of background trees—for color; for contrast; for gate frames; for flower beds; for fall foliage.

Windbreak. If icy cold winds of gale force visit your home during the winter months, you can cut down the damage to weaker shrubs and flowers by planting sturdy specimens of trees in a row for a windbreak.

Screen. Ugly objects can be screened by the judicious planting of certain trees in clusters. In a suburban situation, a screen should be low and well-placed so as not to dominate the yard, but to blend in with it. It should not cut down on air circulation, particularly if it is in the backyard near the recreation area. It should not cut off light, either, especially from garden sites that need sunshine.

OTHER CONSIDERATIONS. Before you select any tree for your property, study these final important points:

Shade. On a hot summer day, a person wants a shade tree under which he can sit or lie or rest. However, total shade in a yard can prevent the growth of flowers, shrubs, and trees. A compromise must be reached before going ahead with planting.

Growth habits. Every tree has a characteristic habit of growth, called its "framework." Take into consideration a tree's framework when you are selecting it either to supplement the architectural lines of a building or to provide a certain landscape value.

Hardiness. Certain trees cannot grow near the sea; others cannot grow in sandy soils; still others cannot grow in cold climates, others in hot climates. It is essential to plant a tree in an area where it is compatible with soil conditions and climatic conditions. Be sure to check the hardiness zone for each tree you consider.

Birch's graceful lines, as well as starkly white bark, make it a standout in any natural setting. Here it blends in with evergreens and deciduous trees, even echoing curve of roadway.

Transplantability. Plant a tree only if you are satisfied that it shall remain there forever. If you must transplant a tree, be sure that you take every precaution not to injure it. Otherwise it may die.

Soil. Because soil conditions vary throughout the country, it is wise to select a tree like those you see growing successfully around you.

Roots. The roots of the willow and the poplar invade drains; don't plant them near septic fields or drain tiles. The oak and hickory are deep-rooted and cannot compete with grass and shrubbery for moisture. The maple and the elm are shallow-rooted, and may wreck grass and shrubs. Shallow-rooted trees can damage sidewalks and street curbs.

Although these spectacular oaks line a walkway in a large city, a column of them would serve as excellent beautification for a side street in a small city or suburb.

Maples serve well as street trees in a crowded metropolis and would not dwarf fairly large homes in a suburban setting. Street trees should not be much taller than this for residential neighborhood.

Large weeping willow forms dramatic background at the rear of this suburban garden.

Although spidery honey locusts line large esplanade of city site, such planting can form excellent windbreak in country or suburban area. Locusts here protect smaller shrubs huddled under them from icy wintry blasts.

Insects and diseases. Avoid trees subject to serious insect pests and/or diseases. For example: the American elm must be sprayed to protect it from the bark beetle; the American sycamore is weakened by anthracnose; the columnar Lombardy poplar can get a canker disease.

Pruning and shearing. Some trees are almost maintenance-free, while others require a great deal of work. Nearly all deciduous trees should be pruned periodically to maintain their suitable form and avoid weak framework, to prevent ice damage in the winter, and to prevent interference with traffic.

Fruit. Some trees grow attractive and colorful fruits. Many fruit trees are grown for their ornamental nature rather than for their fruit. Others are grown for their produce.

Leaf-raking problems. Deciduous leaves fall in the autumn. Whether you want to spend your fall raking up leaves or not may dictate what kind of tree to buy. Modern power mowers have leaf-raking attachments that chop up leaves and make mulch out of them. It is best to remove the leaves from the ground and let them work in the compost heap rather than lie on the ground to decompose there where they may keep sun and moisture away from the grass.

Life expectancy. Some trees last a long time, some die quickly: for example, the oak lives to a ripe old age, a willow is short-lived because of its brittle wood and its susceptibility to disease, and so is the redbud; the sugar maple is a long-lived tree, but the silver maple is short-lived.

HOW TO USE THE TREE LIST. Each tree listed here includes its Common Name, its Botanical Name, its ultimate Height at Maturity, and its Hardiness Zone. In some instances a second common name will be listed in parentheses.

For the convenience of the suburban gardener, the tree list is broken into five sections: one list includes trees that grow to a mature height of over 35 feet; the second includes trees that rarely grow over 35 feet; the third lists ornamental trees arranged according to size and shape; the fourth has trees chosen primarily for color and beauty; the fifth lists special purpose trees. All can be grown in the suburban yard, but some need much more room than others.

Certain evergreens are listed in this chapter, especially large ones that can be used for windbreaks and specimens. Later on, there is a separate chapter on evergreens, one on foundation plantings, edgings, and shrubs, and one on hedges.

Some shrubs are considered trees. For that reason certain names may appear in this chapter *and* in the chapter on shrubs. Likewise, some flowers are considered trees, shrubs, and perennials too. Such specimens appear under trees, shrubs, and flowers.

TREES OVER 35 FEET HIGH

COMMON NAME	BOTANICAL NAME	HEIGHT	HARDINESS ZONE
Acacia, Bronze	*Acacia pruinosa*	60	10
Albizia (Silktree; Mimosa)	*Albizia julibrissin*	36	7
Alder, Italian	*Alnus cordata*	45	5
Ash, European	*Fraxinus excelsior*	120	3
Beech, Weeping	*Fagus sylvatica pendulata*	90	4
Birch, Canoe	*Betula papyrifera*	90	2
Birch, Weeping	*Betula pendula gracilis*	60	2
Birch, River	*Betula nigra*	90	4
Bottletree, Flame	*Brachychiton acerifolium*	60	10
Carob	*Ceratonia siliqua*	50	10
Catalpa, Southern	*Catalpa bignonioides*	45	4
Cedar, Incense	*Calocedrus decurrens*	135	5
Cherry, Amur Choke	*Prunus maackii*	45	2
Chestnut, Chinese	*Castanea mollissima*	60	4
Chinaberry, Umbrella	*Melia azedarach umbraculiformis*	45	7
Crabapple, Siberian	*Malus baccata columnaris*	50	2
Cypress, Lawson False	*Chamaecyparis lawsoniana*	120	5

COMMON NAME	BOTANICAL NAME	HEIGHT	HARDINESS ZONE
Dogwood, Flowering	Cornus florida	40	4
Elm, Chinese	Ulmus parvifolia	50	5
Eucalyptus (Red Gum)	Eucalyptus camaldulensis	150	9
Fir, Douglas	Pseudotsuga mensiesii	200	4–6
Gum, Red Flowering	Eucalyptus filifolia	30–50	10
Hawthorn, Cockspur	Crataegus crus-galli	36	4
Hemlock, Canada	Tsuga canadensis	90	4
Holly, American	Ilex opaca	45	5
Holly, English	Ilex aquifolium	70	6
Hornbeam, American	Carpinus caoliniana	36	2
Hornbeam, European	Carpinus betulus	45	5
Juniper, Rocky Mountain	Juniperus scopulorum	36	5
Larch, European	Larix decidua	105	2
Laurel, California	Umbellularia californica	75	7
Magnolia, Southern	Magnolia grandiflora	40	7
Maple, Norway	Acer platanoides	90	3
Mountain Ash, European	Sorbus aucuparia	45	2
Oak, Sawtooth	Quercus acutissima	45	6
Pecan	Carya illinoensis	150	5
Pine, Austrian	Pinus nigra	90	4
Pine, Ponderosa	Pinus ponderosa	150	5
Pine, Scotch	Pinus sylvestris	75	2
Plum, American	Prunus americana	50	3
Poplar, White	Populus alba	90	3
Poplar, Lombardy	Populus nigra italica	90	2
Redbud, Eastern	Cercis canadensis	36	4
Sassafras	Sassafras albidum	60	4
Spruce, Engelmann	Picea engelmannii	150	2
Spruce, Colorado	Picea pungens argentea	100	2
Sweet-gum	Liquidambar styraciflua	125	5
Sycamore (London Plane-tree)	Platanus hybrida	100	5
Tree-of-Heaven	Ailanthus altissima	60	4
Tupelo, Black (Black Gum)	Nyssa sylvatica	90	4
Walnut, English	Juglans regia	90	5–6

TREES LESS THAN 36 FEET HIGH

Apricot	Prunus armeniaca	30	5
Ash, Velvet	Fraxinus velutina	20–45	7
Blackhaw	Viburnum prunifolium	15	3
Buckeye, Red	Aesculus pavia	18–36	5
Buckthorn, Common	Rhamnus cathartica	18	2
Cherry, Common Choke	Prunus virginiana	30	2

COMMON NAME	BOTANICAL NAME	HEIGHT	HARDINESS ZONE
Crabapple, Flowering	Malus floribunda	30	4
Cornelian-cherry	Cornus mas	24	4
Dogwood, Japanese	Cornus kousa	21	5
Ginkgo (Maidenhair Tree)	Ginkgo biloba	30	4
Golden-chain Tree	Laburnum anagyroides	21	5
Hawthorn, Cockspur	Crataegus crus-galli	36	4
Hawthorn, Lavalle	Crataegus lavallei	21	4
Hawthorn, Paul's Scarlet	Crataegus oxyacantha paulii	15	4
Holly, Chinese	Ilex cornuta	9	7
Holly, Japanese	Ilex crenata convexa	20	6
Horse Chestnut, Ruby Red	Aesculus carnea briotii	35	3
Laburnum, Waterer	Laburnum watereri	30	5
Linden, Mongolian	Tilia mongolica	30	4
Lilac, Amur	Syringa amurensis	30	4
Lilac, Japanese Tree	Syringa amurensis japonica	30	4
Locust, Black	Robinia pseudoacacia umbraculifera	15	3
Loquat, Japanese	Eriobotrya japonica	20	7
Magnolia, Kobus	Magnolia kobus	30	4
Magnolia, Saucer	Magnolia soulangiana	15	5
Magnolia, Star	Magnolia stellata	20	5
Maple, Amur	Acer ginnala	20	2
Maple, Fullmoon	Acer japonicum	25	5
Maple, Almira, Norway	Acer platanoides almira	16	3
Mesquite, Common	Prosopis chilensis	35	9
Mountain Ash, American	Sorbus americana	30	2
Mountain Ash (Rowan Tree)	Sorbus aucuparia fastigiata	35	2
Oak, Engler's	Quercus engleriana	30	7
Oak, Lebanon	Quercus libani	30	5
Oleander	Nerium oleander	20	7–8
Olive, Common	Olea europaea	25	9
Orange, Hardy	Poncirus trifoliata	35	6
Peach, Flowering	Prunus persica	24	5
Pear, Callery	Pyrus calleryana	30	5
Pine, Shore	Pinus contorta	30	7
Plum, Myrobalan	Prunus cerasifera	24	3
Possom Haw	Ilex decidua	30	3
Serviceberry, Apple	Amelanchier grandiflora	25	4
Silverbell, Carolina	Halesia carolina	30	5
Snowbell, Fragrant	Styrax obassium	30	6
Sumac, Shining (Flameleaf)	Rhus copallina	30	4
Viburnum, Siebold	Viburnum sieboldii	30	4
Willow, Babylon Weeping	Salix babylonica	30	6
Willow, Black	Salix nigra	30	6

TREES FOR COLOR AND BEAUTY. The most important reasons for choosing any tree for a suburban lot are its dramatic coloring possibilities. Ornamental trees have been arranged below according to shape and size. Because of the inability of the suburban lot to hold wide-growing trees, you should pay particular attention to columnar and pyramidal trees. Some of them that grow 100 feet and higher can live without trouble in a small lot, since the diametrical width is the only crucial factor in their size.

The six basic shapes. Although there are actually a dozen or more basic shapes in which ornamental and shade trees grow, these are the six basic forms that are recognized as most common:

Umbrella	Pyramidal	Columnar
Weeper	Globe	Spreader

The most versatile for the suburban gardening situation is the *columnar* shaped tree, exemplified by the Olmsted maple and the Washington hawthorn. Columnar shape in a tree is particular practical in a small lot area because the tree at full vertical growth will take up little lateral space. It produces its dimension vertically, giving excellent contrast to the horizontal lines of house and grounds. This up-and-down quality of a columnar tree can be used to excellent advantage as an accent to the flatter shapes of garden and lot.

The *globe* shape is also very useful in a suburban site, particularly to give a special roundness to a certain area. Two examples of globe-shaped trees are the Norway maple and the saucer magnolia. In winter, the globe shape offers a fine contrast to the straight up-and-down lines of trees and shrubs surrounding it.

The *umbrella* type, exemplified by the thornless honey locust and the umbrella chinaberry, adds a great deal of variety to an otherwise vertical and rounded collection of shapes. The cooling psychological effect of the umbrella form lends grace and comfort to a hot summer's day.

The *pyramidal,* like the littleleaf linden and the callery pear, affords a contrasting shape that can be used individually to give a special look to a certain spot in the yard.

The *weeping tree,* popularized as the weeping willow and the cutleaf weeping birch, lends a flowing kind of beauty to an otherwise prosaic selection of foliage. There is an emotional appeal in the sight of a weeping tree, giving a softness and a charm to an otherwise stiff and uncompromising scene.

The *spreader,* like the golden-rain tree and the flowering dogwood, is excellent for providing a background shape behind the house and for giving rounded areas of flowering color to please the eye. Many a spreader has a dramatic trunk and the limb shape inside the silhouette; others have extremely bright blossoms or variegated foliage that play against the common green color and texture of most trees.

With these six basic shapes in mind, you can give your yard a dramatic, eye-arresting look.

The trees listed and described below, incidentally, are only representative and do not include all the types available. And, as has been said before, they are trees that do not grow so big that they totally overpower the yard and everything in it.

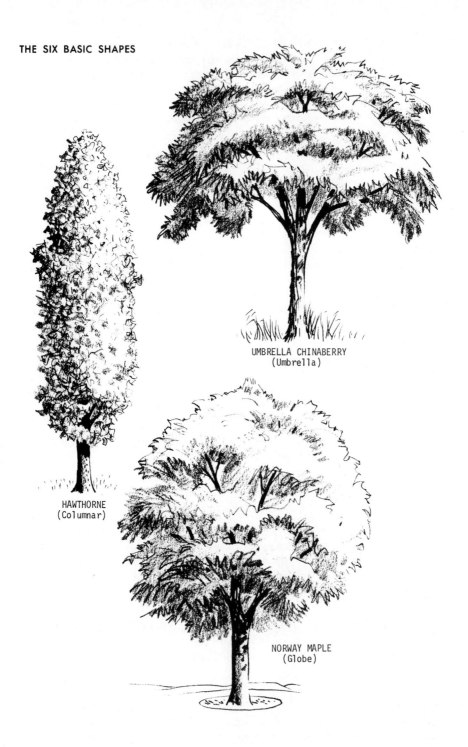

UMBRELLA CHINABERRY
(Umbrella)

HAWTHORNE
(Columnar)

NORWAY MAPLE
(Globe)

FLOWERING DOGWOOD
(Spreader)

CUTLEAF WEEPING BIRCH
(Weeper)

CALLERY PEAR
(Pyramidal)

DECIDUOUS TREES

NAME	HEIGHT	ZONE	DESCRIPTION
Umbrella Trees			
Pink Bud Sargent Crabapple *(Malus sergentii rosea)*	8'	4	Lowest growing of all Crabapples. Pure red fragrant flowers ½ inch and pea-sized red fruits. All flowering crabapples make good small ornamental trees and street trees. Hardy, can be used for windbreaks. Other varieties have different colored flowers and fruits.
Almira Norway Maple *(Acer platanoides almira)*	16'	3	Crisp firm foliage, densely branched round-headed shape, solid silhouette, masses of small yellow flowers in spring—makes effective ornamental specimen. Leaves have distinctive yellow color in fall. Grows rapidly, withstands city conditions; difficult to maintain any growth within area of its roots.
Umbrella Chinaberry *(Melia azedarach umbraculiformis)*	45'	7	Dense foliage, long clusters of lilac flowers in spring, yellow berries in fall (poisonous). Grows rapidly, good shade tree, adaptable to droughty dry soils. Semi-evergreen, will withstand some frost but a short-lived plant.
Weepers			
Weeping Higan Cherry *(Prunus subhirtella pendula)*	30'	5	Small leaves, bright pink blossoms fading to white in summer. Fruits in early summer, pendulous branches. Bushy, hardy, but short-lived.
Japanese Pagoda Tree *(Sophora japonica pendula)*	18'	4	Round head, uneven skirt of branches—good for formal and informal plantings. Useful for shade or street planting; not troubled by insects or diseases. Can be kept to small size with pruning.
Cutleaf Weeping European Birch *(Betula pendula gracilis)*	60'	2	Lacy foliage and distinctive white trunk. Excellent for lining driveway, path or standing by itself. Grows well in moist conditions; will not tolerate dry land. Can be troubled by a leaf miner and birch borer. The River Birch and Gray Birch are short-lived.
Red Jade Crabapple *(Malus purpurea lemoinei)*	25'	4	Pendulous, white blossoms in spring, tiny bright red fruits in summer. Can be specimen in small lot or part of street planting.
Pyramidals			
European Hornbeam *(Carpinus betulus)*	45'	5	Natural pyramidal shape that requires only light pruning. Yellowish in fall; good specimen ornamental, shade tree or for street. Can be pruned to hedge shape. Susceptible to scale; controllable with malathion spray.
Southern Magnolia *(Magnolia grandiflora)*	90'	7	Waxy white blooms, big feathery leaves—excellent early spring-flowering ornamental; primarily lawn plant. In late summer bright red fruits. Hardy tree, can withstand freezing temperatures except where defoliated by wind. Used for background or windbreaks.
Callery Pear *(Pyrus calleryana)*	30'	5	Early spring blossoms followed by small, inedible fruits. Green foliage in summer, plum or glossy scarlet in fall. Tight pyramidal shape. Least susceptible of all pears to fire blight.

NAME	HEIGHT	ZONE	DESCRIPTION
Globes			
Globeheaded European Ash (*Fraxinus excelsior 'Nana'*)	see description	3	Perfect lollipop shape, grows in short rounded mass of foliage which can then be grafted onto trunk of any size. Susceptible to scale; easy to transplant; grows rapidly.
Flowering Globe Locust (*Robina pseudoacacia umbraculifera*)	75'	3	Also known as Black Locust. Weedy tree, recommended in areas where others fail. Flashy pink at end of spring; lacy compound leaves give light and airy shade—good patio tree. Pendulous clusters of small flowers like wisteria. Can be grafted onto smaller trunk for flowering ornamental in small yard.
Ruby Red Horsechestnut (*Aesculus carnea briotii*)	75'	3	Covered with showy flowers in the spring and fruits in the fall. Flowers flaming red over rich green background in pyramidal clusters up to 10 inches in diameter. Fruits and nuts drop when leaves do. Nuts contain bitter poison.
Columnars			
Washington Hawthorn (*Crataegus phaenopyrum*)	30'	4	Clusters of white flowers in May and June; bright green leaves in summer; red fruits in late summer; orange-to-scarlet foliage in fall. This hawthorn one of the last species to bloom.
Olmsted Maple (*Acer platanoides olmsted*)	90'	3	Dense shade tree; stately, upright. Turns bright color (red, yellow, orange or scarlet) in fall.
Sentry Ginkgo (*Ginkgo biloba fastigiata*)	30'	4	Fan-shaped leaves; tree about 7 feet in diameter. Fruits like small plums in fall; foliage turns a brilliant yellow. Plant only male ginkgo, sexually propagated. Female produces foul-smelling fruits.
Spreaders			
Golden-rain Tree (*Koelreuteria paniculata*)	30'	5	Display of small yellow flowers in summer. In fall, shiny, papery pods. Quick-growing but weak and short-lived. Can be ornamental or street tree.
Flowering Dogwood (*Cornus florida*)	40'	4	White blossoms in late May; red berries in fall and foliage turns color. Some varieties have red blossoms, some pink, some cherry. One of the most famous of ornamentals.
Sargent Cherry (*Prunus sargentii*)	35'	4	Deep pink flowers in spring, green in summer. Brilliant red in fall. After leaves drop, small black fruits.

6 | Evergreens

THE EVERGREEN is one of the most versatile plants available to the suburban gardener. Because it does not shed its leaves/needles in the winter but retains its form and texture at a time when everything else turns bare, the evergreen can give a house and grounds a permanently desirable background. The evergreen also affords an amazing variety of shapes, sizes, heights, and widths from which to choose.

Its thickness and habit of growth make the evergreen excellent hedge material. The best varieties of evergreen for hedges are listed in Chapter 9. The evergreen is also an excellent foundation plant, for use in conjunction with the house itself, to enhance its appearance and give needed texture to its exterior. It can even be used in special cases as a ground cover in place of grass.

An evergreen costs more than a deciduous tree or plant, yet you can consider it well worth the extra money inasmuch as you will be able to enjoy it in full leaf throughout the year.

EVERGREEN TYPES. The evergreen has a distinctive shape that remains exactly the same throughout the year. Each species of evergreen has its own shape and/or variety of special shapes. Some of the forms are:

Prostrate or recumbent   Pyramidal
Globular   Conical
Columnar

MAIN SPECIES OF NEEDLE-LEAVED EVERGREENS. There are seven main species of needle-leaved evergreen trees as shown in the following table:

(1) Juniper (*Juniperus*).   (5) Pine (*Pinus*).
(2) Yew (*Taxus*).   (6) Spruce (*Picen*).
(3) Arborvitae (*Thuja*).   (7) Fir (*Abies*).
(4) Hemlock (*Tsuga*).

SPREADING YEW   CREEPING JUNIPER   DWARF YEW   MUGHO PINE   GLOBE ARBORVITAE

Best types of evergreens for slopes, foundation plants, edgings, and low accents.

Mugho dwarf pine (foreground) combines with Japanese andromeda (right) and fragrant viburnum (left) to form especially dramatic foundation planting against rock wall. Ground cover of pachysandra carries out evergreen theme.

Two species of juniper mix with cotoneaster to act as ground cover in preventing rock-strewn bank from eroding onto lawn. Pines above carry out needle-leaved grouping. Juniper and cotoneaster are especially adaptable for use as accents and foundation plants. Dwarf eastern white pine can be planted as specimen in small garden or used with other dwarfs in special grouping.

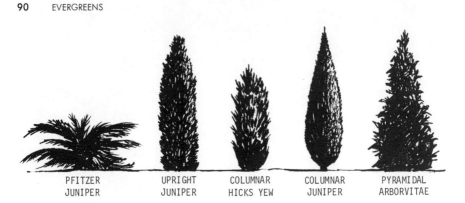

| PFITZER | UPRIGHT | COLUMNAR | COLUMNAR | PYRAMIDAL |
| JUNIPER | JUNIPER | HICKS YEW | JUNIPER | ARBORVITAE |

Evergreens of medium size for tall foundation accents and garden backgrounds.

Evergreens can be combined for a pleasing effect. Here classically trimmed yew in foreground, pyramidal hemlock in background, tall spruce at left act as spectacular border for flagstone steps.

Versatility of broad-leaved ever-green foundation plants is demon-strated by this grouping against stone wall of house. Rhododendron, Japanese andromeda (right), mountain andromeda (left), moun-tain laurel, and pachysandra all blend to form natural mass against rock surface.

Growth of andromeda, leucothoë, and mountain laurel soften harsh lines of outbuilding and adds grace to fall and winter starkness of out-door scene.

UPRIGHT YEW   SPRUCE   CONICAL   SCOTCH PINE
                                     SPRUCE

Large evergreens for background plants, landscape specimens, and wind screens.

Wide-spreading evergreens combine with large deciduous trees to make definitive border for a large lawn planted with flower bed of impatiens.

While birches and dogwoods shed in late autumn and winter months, blue spruce stands firm with shape and texture intact. Blue tint makes spruce excellent foil against green of other needle-leafs.

Stately, pyramidal shape of balsam fir emerges amidst leafless branches around it at wintertime. This tree requires cool, moist conditions for optimum growth.

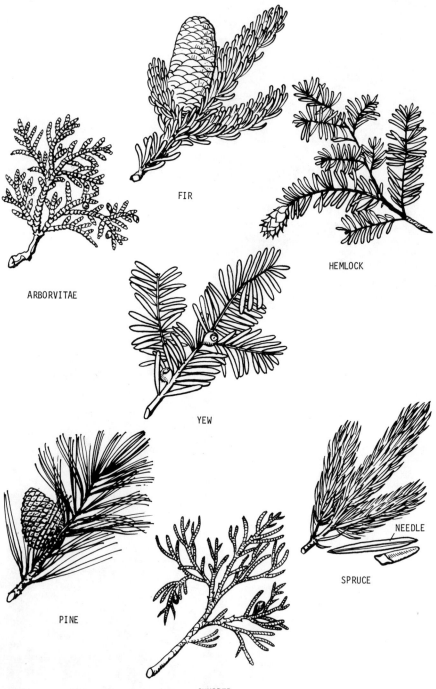

ARBORVITAE

FIR

HEMLOCK

YEW

PINE

JUNIPER

SPRUCE

NEEDLE

Round shape of eastern white pine can be kept only by continuous and assiduous trimming. If unpruned, most evergreens will seek their own shape and size. Long needles shine in sunlight and sparkle in breeze.

Pyramidal American arborvitae grows in classic shape and has soft, velvety texture, making it a perfect individual specimen for any yard or lot.

Huge pyramidal plumed cypress produces dense foliage and fluffy, feathery aspect, making it a good show-off plant.

EVERGREENS

Juniper *(Juniperus)*

Most dependable and versatile of the evergreens. 170 species which can be grown all over the country. Two kinds of needles: juvenile growth sharp and prickly; adult is soft and scalelike. Both types can be on same tree. Female has frosty gray-blue berry. Varies in shape from prostrate ground cover to huge specimen tree. Grows best in open sun and light soil that is not too acid. Needs application of complete fertilizer each year and regular watering first few years. Can be sheared and pruned to control size or for use as hedge. Fast-growing.

COMMON NAME	BOTANICAL NAME	HEIGHT	ZONE	DESCRIPTION
Juniper, Pfitzer	*(Juniperus chinensis pfitzeriana)*	60'	4	Wide-spreading habit, but can be trained to grow upright. Thick, plumelike foliage; useful as foundation plant, individual specimen, entrance tree, banks and slopes. Adaptable to varied conditions; can stand crowding.
Juniper, Prostrate	*(Juniperus chinensis sargentii)*	1'	4	Ground cover.
Juniper, Ames	*(Juniperus chinensis ames)*	60'	4	Pyramidal with steel-blue foliage.
Juniper, Blaauw	*(Juniperus chinensis blaauw)*	60'	4	Blue feathery foliage.
Juniper, Blue Columnar Chinese	*(Juniperus chinensis columnaris)*	60'	4	Silvery green foliage.
Juniper, Pfitzeriana	*(Juniperus chinensis pfitzeriana)*	60'	4	A shrubby versatile shrub.
Juniper, Pfitzeriana Aurea	*(Juniperus chinensis pfitzeriana Aurea)*	60'	4	Golden yellow foliage. Clay soil.
Juniper, Mas	*(Juniperus chinensis mas)*	60'	4	Dense, columnar-shaped.
Juniper, Eastern Red-cedar	*(Juniperus virginiana)*	90'	2	Hardy, very popular.
Juniper, Creeping	*(Juniperus horizontalis)*	12–18"	2	Good in city conditions.
Juniper, Common	*(Juniperus communis)*	2–36'	2	Shrubbery juniper of many heights.

Yew *(Taxus)*

Next to Juniper most adaptable and versatile of evergreens. Over 120 varieties. Very serviceable; thrives in normal site; will survive shade and do well in sun. Stands more soot, air pollution than any other evergreen. Remains glossy in coldest winter. Grows densely; transplants well. Flat blackish-green needles with leathery appearance, pale green underneath. Needles arranged in two flat rows, one on each side of stem. Female bears scarlet, pulpy berries, open at one end. Heights and shapes vary with species.

COMMON NAME	BOTANICAL NAME	HEIGHT	ZONE	DESCRIPTION
Yew, English	*(Taxus baccata repandens)*	60'	5	Hardy species in U. S.
Yew, Canadian	*(Taxus canadensis)*	3–6'	2	Good for shade and hardy, browns in cold.
Yew, Japanese	*(Taxus cuspidata densa)*	50'	4	Hardier than most. One of the best yews.

Arborvitae *(Thuja)*

Staple specimen in America's gardens. Easily rooted, quickly grown; over 50 varieties available. Likes moist areas, thrives on atmospheric moisture. Shows dead branches in areas of long hot summers and extensive periods of drought. Sudden invasion of red spiders can ruin it quickly; other varieties don't age well; branches break off leaving holes that don't heal. Often considered outdated as ornamental. Has lacy flat, fern-like branch with leaf scales overlapping. Has juvenile and adult leaf form. Juvenile is prickly kind of leaf; adult is scale-like one. Distinctive growing habit; puts out flat sprays of leaves. Color varies from deep green to bright golden; size from dwarf to giant. Produces small dried capsules as fruits amongst its leaves.

COMMON NAME	BOTANICAL NAME	HEIGHT	ZONE	DESCRIPTION
Arborvitae, American	*Thuja occidentalis douglas pyramidalis*	60'	2	Narrow, pyramidal, grows tall and fast.
Arborvitae, Oriental	*Thuja orientalis aurea*	30'	6	Globose, low, compact, yellow foliage.
Arborvitae, Beverly Hills	*Thuja orientalis beverlyensis*	50'	6	Columnar to pyramidal, golden tips.
Arborvitae, Blue Spire	*Thuja orientalis howardii*	50'	6	Pyramidal, with blue foliage.
Arborvitae, Siebold	*Thuja orientalis sieboldii*	50'	6	Globe shape to conical, compact and low.

Hemlock *(Tsuga)*

Most graceful of all coniferous evergreen trees growing in North America. Thrives on atmospheric moisture and rainfall; does not do well where there are hot dry summer droughts. Shallow-rooted, transplants easily with ball of soil; takes shearing well and makes excellent clipped hedge. Grows in pyramidal shape with pendulous branches. Needles in rows on each side of twig, slightly bluish beneath and green above. Cones grow at ends of twigs.

COMMON NAME	BOTANICAL NAME	HEIGHT	ZONE	DESCRIPTION
Hemlock, Canadian	*(Tsuga canadensis)*	90'	4	Shears into graceful hedge.
Hemlock, Carolina	*(Tsuga caroliniana)*	75'	4	Ornamental native specimen.
Hemlock, Japanese	*(Tsuga diversifolia)*	90'	5	Dense, rounded, excellent ornamental.
Hemlock, Siebold	*(Tsuga sieboldii)*	90'	5	Dark glossy and dense; fine pyramidal.

Pine *(Pinus)*

One of the most important trees in the world both for lumber it produces and its plentitude of ornamental trees. 77 species being grown today. Larger trees can be mixed with smaller and used in borders, foundation planting and rock gardens. Long needles are bound together in bundles of 2 to 5 and fastened to twig in a tight sheath. Needles are 2 to 5 inches long and cluster at tips of branches.

COMMON NAME	BOTANICAL NAME	HEIGHT	ZONE	DESCRIPTION
Pine, Bristlecone	*(Pinus aristata)*	8'–45'	5	Dwarf types are available.
Pine, Swiss Stone	*(Pinus cembra)*	75'	2	Slow-growing, hardy, fine for small lot.
Pine, Korean	*(Pinus koraiensis)*	90'	3	Very slow growing, good for small gardens.
Pine, Mugho Dwarf	*(Pinus mugo)*	36'	2	From this come many small sizes.

Pine, Jack	*(Pinus banksiana)*	75'	2	Grows on loose dry soil nothing else will grow on.
Pine, Aleppo	*(Pinus halepensis)*	60'	9	Seashore, where other trees fail.
Pine, Norway	*(Pinus resinosa)*	75'	2	Fine ornamental, northeast U.S.

Spruce *(Picea)*

Extremely tall tree, often 100 feet or more at maturity. As it grows, drops lower branches which droop down unattractively. Some dwarf varieties. Extremely hardy. Can be differentiated from other evergreens by examining twig after needles fall off; leave jagged projections on the twigs. Cones hang down. Tree grows upright, pyramidal and has stiff appearance. If crowded, loses lower branches and has ragged appearance.

COMMON NAME	BOTANICAL NAME	HEIGHT	ZONE	DESCRIPTION
Spruce, Colorado	*(Picea pungens)*	100'	2	Needles are green to bluish white.
Spruce, Engelmann	*(Picea engelmannii)*	150'	2	Several good varieties.
Spruce, Oriental	*(Picea orientalis)*	150'	4	
Spruce, Serbian	*(Picea omorika)*	90'	4	"Pendula," has long slender branches.
Spruce, White	*(Picea glauca)*	90'	2	"Densata," the Black Hills Spruce, has bluish green foliage; is hardy.

Fir *(Abies)*

Stately, pyramidal evergreen that grows with horizontal branches at right angles to trunk. Prefers moist, cool climate and high-altitude atmosphere. Of 34 firs in U.S., only few are suitable to environment of suburban garden. Once lower limbs die, no way to force out new growth. Grows in stiff shape with cones upright; needles are soft to touch and blunt; when needles break off, each leaves round smooth scar.

COMMON NAME	BOTANICAL NAME	HEIGHT	ZONE	DESCRIPTION
Fir, Korean	*(Abies koreana)*	54'	5	Comparatively small tree as firs go.
Fir, Nikko	*(Abies homolepsis)*	90'	4	Wide-spreading, good in North U.S.
Fir, Noble	*(Abies procera)*	240'	5	West Coast origin, can grow in East.
Fir, Spanish	*(Abies pinsapo)*	75'	6	Prefers limestone soils, Eastern U.S.
Fir, Veitch	*(Abies veitchii)*	75'	3	Has white undersurface needles.
Fir, White	*(Abies concolor)*	120'	4	Good for suburban landscapes.

7 | Tree Planting and Maintenance

SINCE A TREE CAN BE a fairly important financial investment, you must treat it as a valuable asset to your property. It is as important to the homesite as any element of your house.

Like all living things, a tree needs a great deal of personal attention. Planting, feeding, watering, pruning, and spraying are all extremely important to its welfare. A tree that is neglected will die. You hold the life of every plant on your property in your hands at all times.

HOW TO PLANT A TREE. Almost all trees, dwarfs, and shrubs are planted in a similar manner. Usually when you buy a tree you will receive printed instructions with it; follow these directions carefully.

In general, you should concern yourself with the following when planting a tree:

(1) When to plant
(2) Testing the soil
(3) Knowing what site a tree likes
(4) Preparing the tree
(5) Digging the hole
(6) Arranging the soil
(7) Setting out the tree
(8) Watering the tree
(9) Bracing the tree
(10) Pruning the tree
(11) Mulching the soil around the tree

WHEN TO PLANT. Deciduous trees, those that lose their leaves in the winter, can best be planted in the spring, fall, or winter.

Evergreen trees, those that remain green throughout the winter, can best be planted a little earlier in the fall and later in the spring than deciduous.

Deciduous. In the Northern states the frozen ground of winter makes it difficult to plant the deciduous tree, and so extra precautions must be taken to lessen the shock of water loss and root injury.

Trees with fleshy root systems, like the American hornbeam, beech, butternut, dogwood, golden-raintree, hickory, magnolia, pecan, sassafras, sweetgum, tulip, tupelo, walnut, white fringetree, and yellowwood, are more successfully moved in the spring rather than the fall.

A cold winter following a dry fall can kill a tree planted that fall; to be perfectly safe, you can plant in the spring rather than the fall.

The roots of the deciduous grow even when the soil temperature drops to 45° F. If the tree is planted before the soil gets cold, the roots will grow some even during the first winter months.

Evergreen. The evergreen tree can be planted at any season of the year, with best success during August and early September. However, in colder areas where the tree is exposed to high winds it should be planted in the spring rather than the fall.

Certain evergreens, like the American holly, fir and hemlock, are more successfully planted in the spring rather than the fall.

Generally, the evergreen should be planted when the soil is warm and root growth can continue immediately, as it does in early fall and late spring.

Unlike the deciduous, the roots of the evergreen cease to grow, or grow little, during a dry summer period. If there are late summer or early fall rains, the roots begin to grow again.

TESTING THE SOIL. If you haven't taken a soil test for your lawn, you should make one now. You can buy a do-it-yourself soil-testing kit at your nearest garden store or contact your local agricultural agent.

A test will determine the pH factor (acidity or alkalinity), any need for lime and/or sulphur, and any need for peat moss, humus, or compost.

A slightly acid soil (6 to 7 pH) is best for most trees and plants — but some acid-lovers — Blueberries, Mountain Laurel, Andromeda, Azaleas and Rhododendrons — prefer a pH at about 4.5 or 5.

If the soil tests out too alkaline, add sulphur to it.

If the soil is too acid, add limestone to it.

The fertility or lack of it will dictate whether or not you need to add peat moss or some other kind of humus to give newly-planted trees and shrubs a better chance to grow. In most cases, it is generally accepted practice to add peat in the form of sphagnum or peat moss and/or compost to help nourish the plant roots.

LOCATING THE SITE. A tree or shrub, no matter what kind it is, will grow best in ground that is well-drained, fertile, rich in organic matter, and layered with topsoil. At the same time, most trees and shrubs do *not* like ground that is too light and sandy, too gravelly, too clayey, or badly drained.

PREPARATION OF THE TREE. A tree comes from the nursery ready to plant. It is delivered with bare roots showing, in a tin container, or balled and burlapped.

DIGGING THE HOLE. Amateur gardeners never dig a hole big enough to hold a tree or shrub. In a too-small hole, the roots of the plant bend back toward the main stem where they will not get enough nourishment from the soil to feed the plant. The chances for survival of a badly planted tree are very low.

The hole must be large enough to accommodate the entire ball of earth in a B-and-B (balled and burlapped) wrapping, plus an area around it ample enough to enable the ball to move freely. It must be large enough for all the roots in a bare-root transplant to spread out *fully* in the direction they are growing, plus a clearance of at least 6 to 12 inches.

Do not bend, cramp, or force the roots together to get the plant into a too-small hole. The depth of the hole should be at least 6 to 12 inches deeper than the plant *seems* to need. If you are in doubt about whether or not the hole is deep enough, assume that it is not, and dig it deeper.

ARRANGING THE SOIL. As you dig, sort the soil into separate piles. Place the best soil — that at the top — in one pile, second-best in a second pile, and the poorest soil in a third. Mix in peat moss or compost with the pile of "best" soil. Do the same with the "second-best" pile. Make both these piles as rich as possible. Throw away the third-best pile.

The soil in these two fortified piles is now ready for use after you get the tree into the ground.

SETTING OUT A TREE. A bare-root tree must be planted at once. Tinned trees must be removed from the container, and a B-and-B may be set in, as is, a few days or even a week after delivery.

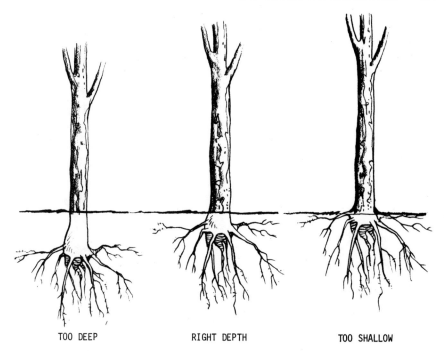

TOO DEEP   RIGHT DEPTH   TOO SHALLOW

Planting bare-root tree at correct depth is important. Soil discoloration line on trunk will show how plant stood at nursery and is proper depth. Illustration shows three trees: left, planted too deep; center, planted just right; right, planted too shallow.

Bare-root tree.

(1) Keep the roots of a deciduous tree from the sun and wind before planting by covering them with soil. Do not prune the top; this has already been done at the nursery.

(2) Loosen the soil at the bottom of the hole; unloosened subsoil can interfere with drainage.

(3) Mix in peat moss and superphosphate to produce a good rich base for the roots.

(4) Make a cone-shaped mound at the bottom of the hole; set the root crown on the mount and spread the roots over and down the sides.

(5) The tree should be seated in the hole with the bud onion, if any, three inches above the level of the hole. If the plant is not grafted or budded, seat it at about the same depth it was, or a little bit higher.

(6) Be sure all the roots are going in the direction of original growth; be sure none of them has been bent or curved inward.

(7) If any roots are damaged or broken, cut them cleanly with a sharp pruning shears or knife.

(8) Take the enriched soil and push it in around the roots, leaving no air at all underground. Add water to eliminate air holes.

(9) Fill the rest of the hole with second-grade soil. Push down on the soil to remove air pockets.

(10) Firm the tree in place by stepping on the dirt around the trunk.

(11) Dig a shallow depression around the tree so the water will collect near the main stem where it is needed.

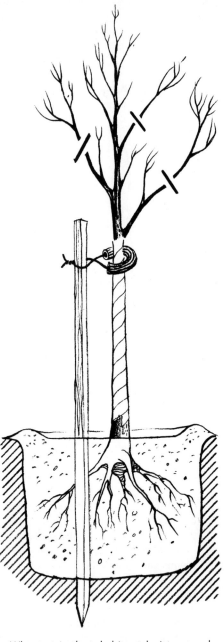

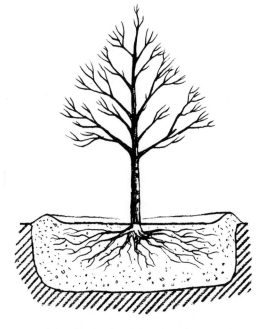

When planting bare-root tree, be sure to spread roots carefully and then pour in dirt. Topsoil should be used, preferably mixed with peat moss.

When tree is planted, drive stake into ground and tie trunk to it for support. Plant stake in direction of prevailing wind and wrap tree in burlap or tree-wrap paper. Prune as shown.

Setting out a B-and-B tree.

(1) Loosen the soil at the bottom of the hole to facilitate drainage.

(2) Mix in peat moss and superphosphate to produce a good rich base for the roots.

(3) Without disturbing the burlap covering on the ball, place the tree in the hole. The top of the ball should be about even with the surface of the ground, or maybe a little lower.

(4) Take the enriched soil and fill it in around the bottom of the ball, half-way up.

(5) Cut the cord that holds the burlap to the trunk. Do not remove the burlap from the ball. The burlap will soon rot in the ground.

(6) Allow water to trickle into the hole until the ball and the soil are thoroughly soaked.

(7) After the water has soaked in, fill up the hole with the rest of the soil, packing in the dirt firmly.

(8) Tamp the soil around the base of the tree.

(9) Give the plant a soaking with water to settle the soil in around the roots and fill in the soft areas.

(10) Irrigate weekly until the tree has made substantial growth. Allow water to run slowly into the root ball for an hour or more at a time. This will prevent the ball from hardening and diminishing the flow of water to the roots.

Birch tree at left is wrapped in tree paper after transplant for protection. Note mulch of wood chips used to keep moisture and warmth in soil around new roots.

In preparing hole for balled-and-burlapped plant, dig it twice size of root ball. Plant ball in humus, preferably mixed with peat moss or bone meal.

Leave burlap on, but cut strings around it. Insert ball so top is at ground level, allowing an inch or two for settling in new dirt. Soak ground before planting.

When balled-and-burlapped plant is in ground, dig trough around trunk to catch water, and then water it first close to newly planted root ball. Fill the secondary trough with water for thorough soaking.

Setting out a tinned tree. The procedure for planting a tinned tree is pretty much the same as the two preceding ones. However, there are a few differences, as:

(1) Dig a hole big enough to hold the container, and twice as wide.

(2) Make sure the soil in the container is moderately moist to hold together and not disturb the roots when you set the tree out.

(3) Place the tree near the hole, and split the two opposite sides of the can with tin snips, chisel, or sharp knife. Pull the sides apart and lift out the ball of soil. A plant in a crimped gallon tin can be removed by tapping the side of the can lightly.

(4) Put the tree in the hole and fill in with topsoil, as in the preceding sections.

WATERING. Water the tree carefully after it has been set in, at least once a week until the plant takes hold and begins to grow on its own.

Do not let it dry out during the summer months, although do not under any circumstances flood it.

Keep the tree watered well for at least two years; after that time most trees and shrubs can take care of their own water needs — except for drought seasons and excessive heat waves. The point is, the trauma of transplant has been overcome by then.

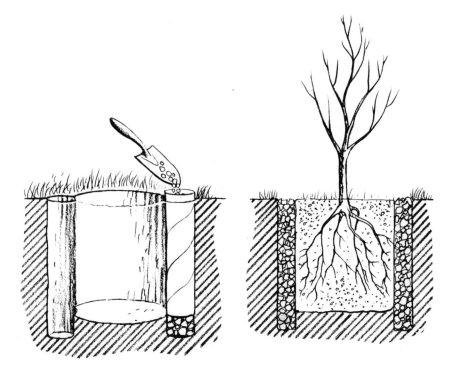

Irrigation holes can be dug on each side of a newly planted tree. Each hole acts essentially as dry well. When filled with crushed rock, holes carry water to the roots.

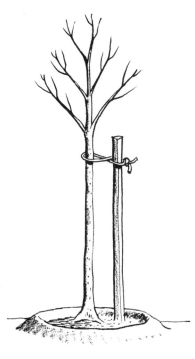

One commercially available tree brace, called Paul's Tree Brace, will keep tree straight in bad weather.

Simple method of staking newly planted tree. Tie figure 8 in rope to prevent tree from leaning in toward stake and loosening rope.

BRACING. Trees and shrubs usually need to be braced against the wind.

If you use wire, slip pieces of old garden hose over the wire where it comes in contact with the tree, and fasten the trunk to the stake in a figure eight.

PRUNING. If the tree came directly from a nursery, you will not have to prune at all. Bare-root plants, tinned plants and B-and-B plants are always pruned for transplant and need not be touched.

Any other tree or plant needs to be pruned upon being moved from one spot to another. The root system has usually been injured by the change of locale. A root system that is greatly reduced in efficiency cannot immediately nourish the plant and provide it with full growth at the top.

In a bare-root transplant—one you make yourself from one part of the garden to another—cut back a third to a half of the foliage exposed. Prune only with a sharp knife or sharp pruning shears.

MULCHING. To keep the soil warm and conserve moisture, pile 2 or 3 inches of mulch around the trunk of a newly planted tree. Mulch will also tend to keep weeds from growing around the tree trunk and stealing nutrient.

For a good mulch use peat moss, rotted leaves, straw, well-rotted manure, or other products from the compost heap. If you have none of these, you can sometimes make do with sand; sand keeps out weeds and allows the soil to absorb the moisture more quickly.

Leave the mulch on all winter the first year in order to allow for as much root growth as possible and to reduce the chances of injury by frost and freezing.

FERTILIZING. It is usually not wise to apply dry commercial fertilizer until new roots are formed to absorb it.

A dilute solution of a balanced chemical fertilizer, however, can be added the first summer after planting.

You can spray the leaves of a newly planted tree with a plant food formulated specially for foliar (leaf) applications. Start when the leaves are half grown and repeat four or five times at ten day intervals.

For tree-feeding after the first year, see the next section of this chapter.

MAINTAINING A TREE. A tree in a forest, in its natural habitat, acquires proper nutrient from dead leaves, dead grass, and dead weeds that rot in the ground and then pass on into the soil to be returned to the tree through its root system.

You must assume that any tree you plant in your yard, or one that was already there when your home was built, will need regular applications of commercial plant food, because it is growing in an unnatural habitat.

WHEN TO FEED. Tree food can be applied in late fall or early spring. In the fall, be sure all growth at the top of the tree has stopped. Some nutrients will enter the roots immediately, and some in early spring before the buds swell.

In the spring, you can feed a tree as soon as the frost is out of the ground. However, as soon as the tree begins to grow, the roots will produce soft succulent tissues

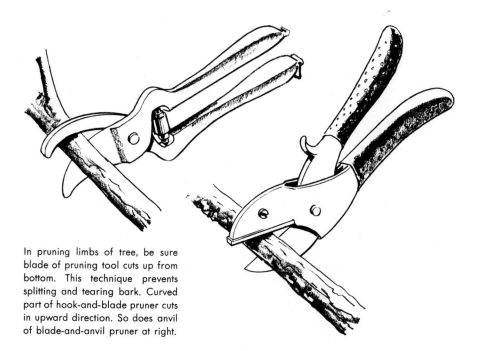

In pruning limbs of tree, be sure blade of pruning tool cuts up from bottom. This technique prevents splitting and tearing bark. Curved part of hook-and-blade pruner cuts in upward direction. So does anvil of blade-and-anvil pruner at right.

With loopers, observe the same rules as with hook-and-blade pruners. The convex edge should always move upward. If hook won't fit at crotch, cut from the side with the blade next to the main branch (right).

which are weak and may be killed in the winter. For that reason, summer feeding is usually unsuccessful.

Vary the frequency of feeding according to the response of the tree. A starving tree should *always* be fed, no matter what the season.

If you observe more than one of the following symptoms of nutritional deficiency in a tree, you may be sure that an application of fertilizer will not harm it.

The leaves are thin or sparse.

The leaves are too yellow during green growth time.

The leaves are undersized in relation to the species.

The tips of the branches tend to die.

The tree has too many dead twigs and branches.

The growth of each twig is abnormally short for the time of the year.

MIX FOR TREE FERTILIZER. For shade trees, ornamentals, and street trees, an ordinary commercial fertilizer mix of either 10-8-6 or 10-6-4 will do for ordinary applications. Most garden supply stores have their own mixes prepared especially for local situations; you can always depend on them for the proper proportions.

Note that small narrow-leaved evergreens can be injured by commercial fertilizer. To feed an evergreen, you should mix nitrogen with an organic carrier first — like 5 pounds of cottonseed meal — and then hoe in or water in the fertilizer on application.

For large narrow-leaved evergreens, you can use commercial mixes.

For broad-leaved evergreens — Azalea, Rhododendron, Laurel, Leucothoë — do not add soil-sweetening fertilizers; use instead acid peat moss and rotted oak leaf mold, mixed in the soil as a mulch. Do not use fresh manure, lime, or wood ash on these plants.

HOW MUCH FERTILIZER TO USE. Although the soil fertility and weather can cause variations, a general formula for deciding how much feed to give a tree is as follows:

(1) For a tree less than 8 inches in diameter, apply at least 1 pound of plant food per inch of the tree trunk's diameter at breast height.

(2) For a tree more than 8 inches in diameter, apply 2 pounds of plant food per inch of the tree trunk's diameter at breast height.

(3) If you maintain organic mulch over the entire root area of the tree, you will not need to apply quite as much plant food as indicated above.

LOCATING THE FEEDING ROOTS. In feeding a growing tree, it is essential to get the plant food as directly as possible to the roots without loss by leaching out (draining away).

The feeding roots of a tree are usually very small — $1/16$ inch in diameter or less. These roots are the only ones that actually take on nutrients and moisture. The larger roots support the weight of the tree.

These small feeding roots occupy an area that is roughly below the outer band of a circular area outside the outermost branches, the width of the band being about two-thirds of the radius of the circle.

The basic problem for the gardener is how to introduce plant food to these feeding roots deep in the ground without losing much of the nutrients in the process.

THE RIGHT WAY TO APPLY PLANT FOOD. There are several accepted methods that gardeners use to apply fertilizer to a tree: surface application, trenching, punch-bar, and needle injection.

Surface application. The least complicated method for feeding a tree is to spread the fertilizer on the surface of the soil beneath the tree. Most of the elements in the fertilizer — particularly phosphorus and potash — remain where they are placed and do not sink into the soil.

After fertilizer has been spread on the surface for several years, the tree will tend to develop more feeding roots toward the soil's surface in order to get the nutrients at the top. In a lawn, the tree roots will interfere with mowing, and will also thin out the grass beneath the tree. Also, a tree with a shallow root system will not weather a dry spell as well as a tree with deep roots. For these reasons, all tree plant foods spread on the surface must be hoed in or watered into the soil thoroughly.

NOTE: Do not apply any dry commercial fertilizer within one foot of a tree trunk, or injury to the root collar and the trunk base will result. Finely pulverized fertilizer mixtures are best for surface feeding.

Trenching. You may prefer to introduce tree food by digging a trench about 2 feet wide in a circle underneath the outer spread of the branches. Fill the trench with compost and soil to which fertilizer has been added. The food reaches the roots more easily than by being hoed in as in surface application.

If grass grows beneath the tree, this method cannot be used. With a shallow-rooted tree, the roots may be cut by the digging. Trenching is only suitable for deep-rooted trees that grow in the open away from lawn.

Holes drilled in ground underneath tree will help get plant food to the feeding roots much faster than letting it soak naturally through ground. Holes should be slanted toward tree trunk, as shown below.

Punch-bar. The most successful method for introducing fertilizer to feeding roots under a tree growing over a lawn is to drill holes in the ground beneath the tree and fill them with food so the nutrients are almost directly applied to the feeding roots.

Each hole should be 1 inch to $1\frac{3}{4}$ inches in diameter, and about 18 to 24 inches deep. The holes should be slanted in toward the tree and should be about 2 feet apart. Drill these holes in the outer two-thirds of the tree's spread, as explained above.

Fill each hole with fertilizer (preferably a granular type), distributing it evenly so that each hole gets the right proportion: then fill the hole with loosely packed peat moss, shredded manure, or topsoil.

To dig the holes you can use an ordinary crowbar; however, this hand work is back-breaking. You can rent a specially made punch-bar at your garden supply center. This bar is punched down into the earth, and when withdrawn brings up the dirt with it.

A soil augur, which is made for use with a regular $\frac{1}{4}$-inch power drill, will supply an 18-inch hole in the soil without compacting the side of the hole.

For a 24-inch hole, you can get an augur for use with a $\frac{3}{8}$- or $\frac{1}{2}$-inch drill. Use a slow-speed drill if possible. You can punch out a full 24-inch hole in half a minute with a power drill.

Needle injection. This is the most efficient method for introducing plant food to feeding roots and is used by professional tree men. Several commercial tree-feeders are available for this operation: they are called "feeding needles" or "feeding guns."

You place the plant food in dry or water solution in the cartridge of the feeder or gun, attach the long needle to a water hose, and turn on the water. The pressure forces the fertilizer through the needle and into the soil as you push the nose of the needle down into the soil.

This tree feeder needle is attached to a garden hose with capsules of fertilizer inserted in gun at top of rod. Insert rod into soil below longest, lowest branches, plunging it full depth into earth. Make holes every two or three feet around an imaginary circle.

Ross Root Feeder

Fertilizers in liquid form are more evenly distributed through the soil than fertilizers in other forms. However, liquid fertilizers do not improve the richness of the soil by adding any organic matter as does dry fertilizer.

INORGANIC FERTILIZERS: WARNING! The use of inorganic fertilizers may cause a severe burning of tree roots if applied in feeding holes. Only use inorganic plant food in the spring, particularly those formulations that contain minor elements that may be needed in special situations.

WATERING. In a compacted soil, neither moisture nor air can penetrate to the tree roots. Trees growing above compacted soil need a great deal more water than those growing above untrodden soil.

Frankly, you will not do much good by watering the surface of the ground with a hose or sprinkler. The moisture simply will not penetrate deeply. To be effective, water must sink at least 8 to 10 inches below the surface of the earth.

To irrigate a tree and insure correct penetration of moisture, you should allow the water to stand in a basin dug around the trunk for several hours, perhaps as much as a day.

If you have to use a sprinkler or hose, allow it to run until an inch of more of water has been applied to the root area.

If you water through an injector-type applicator, moisten the soil thoroughly at each point of injection. It may take fifteen to thirty minutes per hole, depending on the texture of the soil.

PRUNING. The best time to prune a deciduous tree is when the plant is in its dormant state, that is, any time after the leaves have fallen and before the sap begins to rise the following spring. However, certain experts claim that healing callus development is better on wounds made between February 15 and May 15. Evergreens should be pruned in late spring or early summer, just before the big growth starts.

Pruning Tips — Deciduous Trees.

(1) Always have the right equipment: pruning shears, lopping shears, pole pruners, pruning saw. The larger the tree, the more important the proper tools are. (See Chapter 12 on Garden Tools.)

(2) Make each pruning cut with care and do not tear or strip off any bark.

(3) Coat all pruning cuts with non-cracking, long-lasting tree dressing—like the asphalt-varnish type available at most gardening supply stores. This dressing seals the wound until it heals over, and protects the broken wood from fungus infection.

(4) Do not prune too heavily in one year after not touching the tree for some time. If you do, you will have to remove a lot of "sucker" growth next year.

(5) Do not cut limbs so as to leave stubs. A stub will not heal over, and the end can rot. A large stub will provide a channel for wood-rotting fungus to enter the heartwood of the tree.

(6) Smooth over all pruning cuts with a pruning knife. Shape the cuts elliptically, then coat any over ½-inch in diameter with tree dressing.

(7) Prune out the lower branches of a growing tree; low branches restrict the sunlight, kill grass, and prevent good air circulation.

(8) To help the tree retain its desired form, remove some branches other than the lower ones. Keep the horizontal habit of growth of the hawthorn, dogwood, and such trees. Prune in moderation on thin-barked trees like maples and beeches. Thin out ash trees that have become too thickly branched.

(9) Shape tall-growing trees before they reach the maximum permissible height so they do not need to be topped. Never top a tree unless it is absolutely too tall for its location.

(10) Avoid late-summer pruning. Such work may stimulate fall growth in both needle- and broad-leaved evergreens and cause them to be injured in freezing weather.

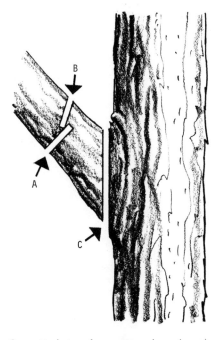

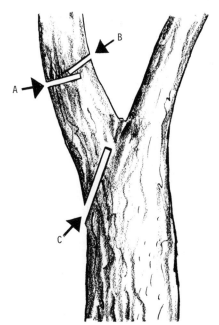

Correct technique for pruning a large branch prevents a tree from becoming infected. Make preliminary undercut at A. Make second cut at B, severing the branch and thus removing weight. Remove remaining stub by cutting at C.

To remove V-shaped crotch, make preliminary cut at A, and secondary cut at B, getting rid of whole branch first. Make cut at C, slanting upward toward point of union of two limbs.

Pruning tips — evergreens.

(1) When shearing *hemlock*, be sure to cut the longest branchlets. This will force the new growth to spread sideways.

(2) When trimming *arborvitae*, disjoint the growth at one of the stem points. Shear in the late spring. The growth will cover the cuts.

(3) Trim *yew* shoots in the late spring, using hand pruners except where you wish to keep long level lines of hedge. Use a power trimmer in that instance.

(4) To make a *fir* branch out, nip the central bud from the tip of the shoot with your thumb and finger.

(5) To replace a broken leader on any needle-leaved *evergreen,* tie the side branch upright on a splint.

(6) In trimming a *fir* or *spruce,* do not allow two leaders to grow out from the same point. Cut off the new one or it will vitiate the other.

(7) To keep *pine* growth dense, nip the central shoot at least halfway back to the branch. Secondary buds will grow from the terminal.

(8) To keep any *evergreen* from winter drying (in February and March), give it a light shearing along the side exposed to wind and sun.

Electric shrub trimmer can be used to good advantage in pruning back most evergreens. Blades move back and forth, cutting on both sides of the blade.

(9) In pruning *pine, spruce* and *cedar* be careful not to cut off any dormant bud, or you will stop further growth of the branch. Never cut off all the green needles on a branch.

(10) Prune back all needle-leaved evergreens except hemlock.

CURING TREE TROUBLES. Although it is advisable for you to plant only trees that do not become susceptible to diseases or insect problems, you may find that even the most rugged do succumb to certain ailments. If, however, a tree is subject to numerous attacks of disease, it is an indication that it is basically unhealthy. It may be planted too deeply or the roots may have rooted because of poor subsurface drainage.

The average spraying equipment available to a suburban homeowner will not reach more than 15 to 25 feet off the ground. If you have higher trees it is advisable to hire a professional sprayer rather than buy more expensive equipment.

Deciduous trees. The most common health problems are:
(1) Gall aphids.
(2) Scale insects and borers.
(3) Leaf-eating insects.
(4) Aphids and mites.
(5) Scorch.

Although *Gall aphids* are terribly annoying, they do not come back year after year the way some other pests do. Nor do they harm the trees at all; they simply disfigure them by causing gall-like growths on the leaves and twigs. An early spring spray will keep them under control: lindane, endosulfan, malathion, phosphamidon, nicotine, pyrethrum.

Scale insects increase in number and drain a tree's vitality. Spray in the early spring, before growth starts, with white-oil emulsion or lime-sulphur diluted for dormant spraying. To kill the young insects before they attach themselves to the bark, spray with malathion; apply 2 sprays about 10 days or 2 weeks apart, starting when the leaves are very short.

Borers cut off the flow of sap from the roots and weaken the tree structurally. To prevent borer attack, spray the trunk and lower branches with endosulfan, beginning the middle of May. Spray once a month through September 15. If borers attack, cut them out with a sharp knife, trim the edges of the wound back to green bark, and paint the wound with tree-wound dressing.

Leaf-eating insects disfigure trees season after season, in some cases completely defoliating the trees and weakening them structurally. Some trees never do recover. Spray with lead arsenate or other formulations to keep these pests in control.

Aphids and *Mites* are tiny sucking insects that weaken trees, deform new growth, and sometimes deform the foliage. They exude a sticky substance called "honey dew," which can cause the development of sooty mold, a black, sticky fungus growth. Spray with lindane, benzene hexachloride, endosulfan, malathion, and so on.

Scorch is a physical condition in a tree caused by drought or some other unfavorable situation. The edges of the leaves become brown. Smog produces a somewhat similar effect on the foliage and growth of certain varieties of trees. There is nothing much you can do except remove the causative factors.

When massive insect infestation is a problem, spray a protective coating on the foliage to kill the bug when it arrives. Time your spraying to maintain a protective coating throughout the season. Shorten the intervals between applications in the spring when growth is rapid; lengthen them in the summer and fall.

Evergreens.

The most common health problems are caused by sucking insects. Certain insects like the aphid, the spruce mite, the pine-leaf mite, and the red spider, can do great harm to individual evergreens during the winter months. These pests pierce the wood and suck out all the moisture in the tree, causing great damage.

Spray the evergreens in late fall with an insecticide like diazinon, lindane, or malathion. Do a careful job and be sure to read the directions on the spray can in order not to over-spray or in any other way mis-use the chemicals in it.

WINTER PROTECTION. In areas where heavy snowfall is usual, prune all trees so that the branches can withstand the weight of piled snow and ice. In windswept areas, you may have to protect young trees with guy wires until their roots become firmly established. Windbreaks provide additional protection.

Winter burn. Winter winds in dry areas may tend to dry out the foliage of deciduous trees; use an anti-desiccant spray to protect the wood.

Because an evergreen doesn't drop its leaves in the winter, it continues to be subject to action by the wind and sun. An ordinary plant evaporates water to the sun's heat in the normal course of the growing season.

Winter sun and winter wind can cause excess evaporation of the water from the evergreen's leaves. With the ground frozen, the tree cannot obtain moisture from the soil to replace that lost to the sun and wind. If *too* much water evaporates, the evergreen can suffer from winter burn, or desiccative drying out.

To prevent the possibility of winter burn, water the evergreen plant well before winter freezes the ground. The extra supply of water underground will aid the plant in surviving the winter without excessive trouble.

Snow load. Too much weight on any branch—even on the evergreen's flexible growth—will break it. There are two ways to cut down on branch breakage due to snow load:

(1) Put boards under the branches to prop them up from the ground.

(2) Tie branches that hang away from the mass of the tree closer to the trunk with strips of cloth.

NOTE: Never plant an evergreen next to the house where it will catch the weight of icicles falling from the roof edges, or where it will receive great slides of melting snow from the roof when thaw sets in.

Winter Bruise. Certain branches will break during winter storms, either from the load of the snow or from the force of the wind.

Bandage these wounds as soon as you see them. Use long strips of cloth or burlap 3 inches wide, and proceed as you would to bandage an arm or a leg. Wind the burlap strips spirally around the branch. Splint it if the branch is in danger of breaking off completely.

If necessary, support splint and bandaged limb with a piece of wood propped on the ground.

Sun and wind burn. The evergreen is subject to burning from the wind and sun as much as any human being. To keep winter sun and wind from harming a young plant, build a shield for it out of burlap, or out of wooden planks.

For a larger tree, make a V-shaped shelter and erect it on the south side of the plant to cut off the sun and wind. Or put a three-sided shelter around the tree, making sure none of the sides touches the branches. The shield can be made of burlap, bamboo stockade, or wooden slats nailed together.

Weather changes. Alternate freezing and thawing affects all trees adversely by shifting the ground around the roots and disturbing the positioning of the plant.

To prevent freezing-thawing troubles, put a 3- to 6-inch mulch of dry leaves and rotted manure under the tree to help the plant through the cold weather.

Extend the mulch out beyond the spread of the roots. Use leaves that will not blow away. If you are subject to high ground winds that may disturb the surface of the landscape, lay boards on the leaves like spokes radiating out from the tree. This protection will tend to keep the leaves from moving about.

In the spring, work the manure into the ground as fertilizer. As soon as the frost gets out of the ground take away all the other materials still there under the tree.

TREE INJURIES. Careless gardening practices can cause a number of serious tree injuries. An injury to a tree's bark is one of the easiest ways to lay it open to further trouble. Even banging a lawn mower into a tree trunk can cause canker later. A pet cat may shred the bark of a tree so badly that it no longer serves as a protective coating and allows the entrance of disease and wood-rotting funguses. Rabbits, mice and other animals can injure young trees in winter by nibbling the bark.

Use chemical repellants to protect trees from rabbits and deer.

The careless use of herbicides can injure trees, too. Keep in mind the following precautions: use herbicides so that they only wet the foliage of the weeds to be eradicated; use low volatile spray materials and apply them when the air is still; use materials that are specific or selective in their killing power.

Tree splits. Most trees are able to close any splits that develop after branches break or V's split after an increase in growth. However, if the split has not healed by the following winter, you should tie the tree halves together with a rope. Then, using a portable winch or a block and tackle rig, draw the rope tighter around the tree until the two halves are fitted together as closely as possible.

Now fasten the halves permanently by drilling two holes through both halves and passing two rods through the holes, with the rods aligned horizontally. Threaded rods for this purpose are available at garden supply stores and nurseries. A $5/8$-inch rod is adequate for a medium sized tree; a $7/8$-inch rod is available for a very heavy tree. When in place, you simply fasten nuts to the end to bolt the halves together permanently.

If the split remains partly open, seal it with heavy asphalt, or a special tree-sealing preparation. Trowel on the asphalt. If the gap is wide, pour sand into it as a base for the asphalt. Seal the gap completely or infection may result.

Do not tie cables, chains, wires or iron straps *around* any tree; the loop will prevent further growth and will strangle the tree.

Lightning damage. Lightning does strike trees continually. The taller and more stately trees are the most susceptible to lightning, of course. So are isolated trees, or scattered specimens.

Damage depends on how deeply the bolt plows into the tree. It may strip a shallow layer of bark from the trunk, top to bottom. The heat of the lightning bolt can kill sapwood.

When examining a lightning-struck tree, wait several days before checking it out. If there is surface damage evident, remove the loose bark, smooth over the rough edges, and use tree dressing on the damaged area.

Smog injury. The unburned portion of gasoline and diesel oil — called smog — affects plants as well as human beings. Certain plants are more affected by smog than others, and some species are immune to it.

Susceptible to smog injury are most species of the pine family, sugar maple, sourgum, sweetgum, and honey locust. Resistant to a certain degree are white fir, incense cedar, and coast live oak. Tolerant are ailanthus, horse chestnut, hackberry, American ash, ginkgo, poplar, sycamore, willow, linden, and elm.

Salt Injury. Salt used as a de-icer during the winter months can prove injurious to trees planted alongside roadways. It is therefore wise to plant trees 30 to 50 feet from the edge of the road. Since this is impractical for the average suburban homeowner, the best solution may be to plant only salt-resistant trees near the street.

Among trees deemed tolerant to salt by agronomist Edward F. Button of the Connecticut Bureau of Highways are: pfitzer juniper, creeping juniper, Adam's needle, privet, tartarian honeysuckle, black locust, honey locust, Russian olive, squaw bush, and tamarix.

Moderately tolerant are thornless honey locust, most oaks, forsythia, weigela, silver buffalo berry, golden willow, ponderosa pine, and green ash.

8 | Flowering Shrubs

SMALLER PLANTS, LIKE DWARF trees and shrubs, can set off the average homesite in many different ways.

One of the most vital is in providing needed color. In fact, the flowering shrub is the single most effective material the suburban homeowner has at his disposal to provide exactly the right accent to the overall picture of his house.

The shrub can also be used effectively as a land divider, a background, or a screen —in other words, as a hedge. Placed as a foundation planting, the shrub enhances the structural lines of a house.

The shrub as hedge and foundation plant will be covered in a later chapter. Here we will deal with the flowering shrub.

FLOWERING SHRUBS. Although a complete list of flowering shrubs would be impossible to undertake in a book like this, it is a good idea to know the particular genuses of plants that can be used for decorative purposes in your garden.

While not intended as being comprehensive, the following list, alphabetized according to the Latin name, will give you one or two species of the main genuses used for flowering shrubs.

FLOWERING SHRUBS

COMMON NAME	BOTANICAL NAME	HEIGHT	ZONE	BLOOMS	COLOR
Almond, Flowering	Prunus triloba	15'	5	Spring	Pink, rose-like flowers
Azalea, Flame	Rhododendron calendulaceum	9'	5	June	Yellow-orange to reddish-orange colors
Azalea, Mollis Hybrid	Rhododendron kosterianum	5'	5	Late May	Hybrid colors include fire-red, poppy-red
Azalea, Rutherford Hybrid	Rhododendron rutherfordiana	6'	7	May	White
Bridalwreath	Spiraea prunifolia	9'	4	Mid-May	White flowers; red-orange foliage in fall
Buddleia, Asian	Buddleia asiatica	2–6'	8–9	April, May	White flowers
Bunchberry	Cornus canadensis	9'	2	May, June	White flowers, red berries
Butterflybush	Buddleia davidii	15'	5	August	White, pink, and purple
Butterflybush, Oxeye	Buddleia davidii magnifica	15'	5	August	Dark blue, with striking orange eye
Camellia, Common	Camellia japonica	45'	7	October–April	Hybrid colors include red, pink, white
Camellia, Sasanqua	Camellia sasanqua	20'	7–8	September–December	Hybrid colors include pink, rose, red, white
Chaste-tree	Vitex agnus-castus	9'	6–7	July–Sept.	Lilac or pale violet blossoms
Cherry, Chinese Bush	Prunus japonica	4'	2	Spring	White and/or pink flowers

118

Flowering quince not only bears flowers that are white, pink, orange, or red in May, but fruit as well. This shrub is thorny and can be sheared and used as a hedge, or can serve as a specimen plant.

Viburnum acts as edging plant along paths and drives, producing a small white flower followed by a bright red fall berry. Snowball plant is a species of viburnum.

Mountain laurel blooms with white, pink, and even red flowers about mid-June and serves as excellent foundation planting year-round. At left leucothoë, also of heather family, has white, waxy flowers in early June, and its leaves turn a beautiful bronze in fall and winter.

COMMON NAME	BOTANICAL NAME	HEIGHT	ZONE	BLOOMS	COLOR
Cherry, Sand	*Prunus pulila*	7'	2	Spring	Long white flowers; black cherries
Cherry-laurel	*Prunus laurocerasus shipkaensis*	9'	5	Spring	White blossoms
Coralberry	*Symphoricarpos orbiculatus*	3–6'	2	Spring	Yellow flowers; purple berries
Crabapple, Japanese Flowering	*Malus floribunda*	30'	4	Early May	Pink-red blossoms
Crabapple, Sargent	*Malus sargentii*	8'	4	Spring	Fragrant flowers
Crabapple, Redbud	*Malus zumi calocarpa*	25'	5	Early May	Pure white
Currant, Clove	*Ribes odoratum*	6'	4	May	Yellow flowers; black berries
Daphne, Burkwood	*Daphne burkwoodii*	6'	5	May	Creamy white to flushed pink blossoms
Daphne, Lilac	*Daphne genkwa*	3'	5	April or May	Blue, lilac-type flowers
Daphne, Winter	*Daphne odora*	4–6'	7	March, April	Fragrant, rosy flowers
Deutzia, Kalmia	*Deutzia dalmiaeflora*	6'	5	May	Cup-shaped carmine flowers
Deutzia, Lemoine	*Deutzia lemoinei*	7'	4	Late May	Single white flowers
Deutzia, Showy	*Deutzia magnifica*	6'	5	Mid-June	Double white flowers
Dogwood, Flowering	*Cornus florida*	40'	4	May	White flowers, red berries
Dogwood, Siberian	*Cornus sibirica alba*	9'	2	Late May	Yellow-white flowers
Elder, American	*Sambucus canadensis*	12'	3	June	White flowers, blue berries
Elder, Scarlet	*Sambucus pubens*	12–24'	4	Mid-May	Yellow-white flowers
Forsythia, Dwarf	*Forsythia vididissima broxensis*	2'	5	April	Profuse yellow blooms
Forsythia, Korean	*Forsythia ovata*	4'	4	April	Bright yellow flowers
Forsythia, Weeping	*Forsythia suspensa*	9'	5	Early spring	Wide arching branches
Gooseberry, English	*Ribes uva-crispa*	3'	4	Spring	Greenish flowers; red berries
Hawthorn, Washington	*Crataegus phaenopyrum*	30'	4	Mid-June	White flowers, scarlet fruit
Heather	*Calluna vulgaris*	18"	4	August through October	Many colors; white, pink, red
Henry St. John's-wort	*Rosa primula*	8'	5	Early bloom	Light-yellow single flowers
Hills of Snow	*Hydrangea arborescens grandiflora*	3'	4	June, July	Heavy flowers
Honeysuckle, Box	*Lonicera nitida*	6'	7	Mid-April	White flowers; very good for hedges
Honeysuckle, Coralline	*Lonicera chrysantha*	12'	3	May, June	Pale yellow flowers
Honeysuckle, Tatarian	*Lonicera tatarica*	9'	3	April	Pink-to-white flowers

COMMON NAME	BOTANICAL NAME	HEIGHT	ZONE	BLOOMS	COLOR
Honeysuckle, Winter	*Lonicera fragrantissima*	6'	5	Mid-April	Fragrant flowers
Hydrangea, Bigleaf	*Hydrangea macrophylla*	12'	5–6	June	Enormous flowers; blue, pink, white
Hydrangea, Smooth	*Hydrangea arborescens*	3'	4	Early summer	Creamy-white blooms
Laurel, Mountain	*Kalmia latifolia*	30'	4	Mid-June	Pink and white flowers
Lilac, Dwarf Korean	*Syringa palibiniana*	3'	5	May	Lilac color
Lilac, French Hybrid	*Syringa vulgaria*	20'	3	May–June	Hybrid colors include: magenta, violet, red-mauve, double white, dark blue
Lilac, Japanese Tree	*Syringa amurensis japonica*	15–20'	4	Mid-June	Creamy white clusters of flowers
Lilac, Persian	*Syringa persica*	6'	5	Late May	Profuse light violet blooms
Magnolia, Purple Lily	*Magnolia liliflora nigra*	9'	6	May	Reddish purple flowers
Magnolia, Saucer	*Magnolia soulangiana*	15'	5	Summer	Vari-colored flowers
Magnolia, Star	*Magnolia stellata*	20'	5	Late April	White double flowers
Meadowsweet	*Spiraea latifolia*	4'	2	June–August	White to pink flowers
Mockorange, Sweet	*Philadelphus coronarius*	9'	4	Spring	Single, very fragrant, flowers
Pearlbush, Common	*Exochorda racemose*	9'	4	May	Small white flowers
Quince, Flowering	*Chaenomeles speciosa*	6'	4	May	Varieties of white, pink, red, and orange
Quince, Japanese	*Chaenomeles japonica*	3'	4	Early May	Red and/or orange blossoms
Redbud	*Cercis chinensis*	10'	6	Mid-May	Rosy-purple flowers
Rhododendron, Catawba	*Rhododendron catawbiense*	6'	4	May	Lilac to white color
Rose, Damask	*Rosa damascena*	6'	4	Summer	"Trigintipetala" has semi-double red flower
Rose, Father Hugo	*Rosa hugonis*	7'	5	Late May	Single canary-yellow flower 2 inches across
Rose, Moyes	*Rosa moyesii*	9'	5	Mid-June	Blood-red single flower 2½ inches across
Snowball, Chinese	*Viburnum macrocephalum*	12'	6	May	Largest of flower clusters
Snowball, Fragrant	*Viburnum carcephalum*	9'	5	May	Fragrant white flower clusters, followed by berries
Snowberry	*Symphoricarpos albus laevigatus*	6'	3	Mid-June	Pink flowers; white berries
Spicebush	*Calycanthus occidentalis*	9'	6	Mid-May	Red-brown flowers
Thorn, Cockspur	*Crataegus crus-galli*	36'	4	May	White flowers, red fruit

HOW TO PLANT A SHRUB. The procedure for planting a shrub is exactly the same as the procedure for planting a tree, as has been described already in the section under trees.

HOW TO TRANSPLANT A SHRUB. Oftentimes, when you suddenly have a brand-new "concept" of what your garden should look like, you will wonder whatever possessed you to put a yew in this spot, or a juniper in that!

The only answer is to move it where it should be—or where you *now* think it should be.

You can do your own transplanting, but you must pay attention to several important rules while you do the moving:

(1) Dig a circular trench around the shrub or tree you want to move, keeping it at least an inch away from the trunk. The circular trench should be about 6 to 8 inches wide and deep enough to go down beneath the roots.

(2) With a fork or spade, shape a ball of earth around the roots, cutting down and chopping off excessively long ones with a sharp knife.

(3) Now get the spade in under the ball of earth and trim it so all roots are either cut or are in the ball under the trunk.

(4) Tip the tree over on its side, lifting the ball of earth up out of the newly-made hole. Place a roll of burlap sacking under the ball inside the hole.

(5) Unroll half the burlap under the ball, and tip the plant back the other way. Unroll the other half under the ball.

(6) Bring all four corners of the burlap up and tie them together by punching string through the burlap and fastening the ends around the trunk.

(7) If the burlap is loose, tie it with a ball of string or rope.

(8) Use another strip of burlap and wrap it around the base of the plant. The trunk must be protected from bruises.

(9) Dig a slanting trench to one side of the hole under the ball.

(10) Tip the ball up, and slide a section of plywood, or a platform of planking in under the ball, and pull the plant back onto the platform.

(11) Drag the platform and plant up the slanting side to ground level.

(12) Take the plant to its new site and follow planting instructions.

You can handle trees up to 6 inches in diameter this way. The smaller the tree or shrub, the easier it is to move and the quicker it will recover from the shock of transplantation.

Do not try to move trees with a diameter of more than 7 or 8 inches. That kind of transplanting job takes know-how—and the proper equipment.

HOW TO PROPAGATE PLANTS THREE WAYS. Transplanting a tree or shrub is not the answer to a landscaping problem when you want three or four shrubs exactly like one you already have. It is possible to propagate a new shrub or shrubs from the one you already have without resorting to the use of seed-planting and its attendant problems.

There are several methods for propagating a plant from a growing specimen: cutting or slips, layering, and grafting.

Some plants are difficult to propogate by cuttings or by layering: fir, hemlock, locust, red-cedar, mimosa, redbud, ginkgo, mountain laurel, golden-rain tree, blue spruce, myrica, and andromeda. Most others, however, can be layered.

To achieve success, be sure to use only healthy plants, propagate in the right

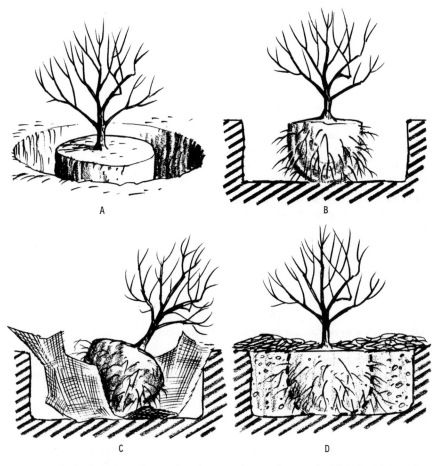

To prepare shrub for transplanting, first dig a circular trench around it (**A**). When the trench is deep enough, free the shrub from the ground below with a spade (**B**). Tip the plant to one side and slide burlap under the roots. Then tip the plant to the other side and pull the burlap under entire ball of earth (**C**). Lift balled-and-burlapped plant out and replant it at same depth in prepared hole (**D**).

season, protect the plants from drying out, and give new plants extra care until established.

CUTTINGS. A cutting, sometimes called a slip, is simply a branch cut from a living tree or shrub and set out to root by itself. Cuttings from roses and spring-flowering shrubs should be made in midsummer before the new stems are hard but are no longer succulent. Cuttings from evergreens—holly, yew, arborvitae and juniper— root best in the late fall or early winter after the first heavy frosts. Cuttings from boxwood can be taken anytime.

A successful cutting will form roots within two months. Midsummer cuttings should be rooted by fall; winter cuttings should be rooted by spring. Although a cutting roots quickly, it needs a coldframe for the intermediate days between rooting and planting.

Materials needed.
(1) 6-inch flower pot.
(2) Polyethylene (plastic) freezer bag.
(3) Peat moss and clean sand.
(4) Rooting stimulant.

A rooting stimulant is a preparation of organic chemicals developed to hasten the formation of roots on cuttings, slips, and layers. Such a preparation is available at garden supply stores.

How to make a cutting root. The easiest and most familiar way to make a cutting take root is to plant it in a flower pot covered with a plastic freezer bag. Follow these easy steps:

(1) Prepare a rooting medium by mixing clean sand with an equal part of peat moss.

(2) Moisten the mixture until you can squeeze a few drops of water out of it by hand. If too much water squeezes out, the mix is too wet; add peat moss and sand to dry it.

(3) Fill a 6-inch flower pot with the rooting medium.

(4) Make a slanting cut 2 to 6 inches from the tip of the branch you want to plant.

(5) Strip the leaves from the lower half of the cutting and dip the base of the cutting in the rooting stimulant.

(6) Insert the cutting to about half its length in the potted rooting medium. You can plant more than one cutting to a pot. A 6-inch pot will hold ten to twelve slips.

(7) Spray the cuttings lightly with water.

(8) Place a polyethylene freezer bag completely around the flower pot. Twist the top closed and fasten it with a rubber band.

Carry newly removed cutting from one place to another in polyethylene freezer bag.

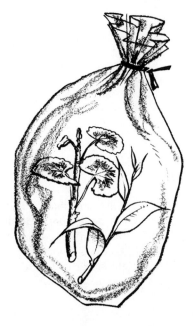

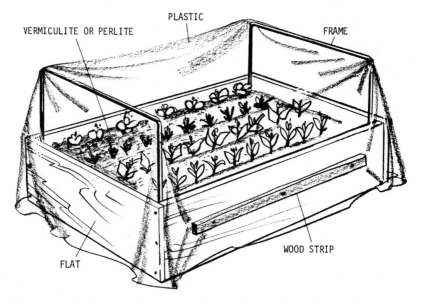

VERMICULITE OR PERLITE

PLASTIC

FRAME

FLAT

WOOD STRIP

Cuttings must be covered and protected while they take root. Use well-drained rooting medium for soil, such as vermiculite or perlite. Cover the frame with polyethylene and nail it in
place with a wood strip.

(9) Set the cuttings in a window where they are exposed to daylight but never to
direct sunlight.

(10) After the cuttings have been in the flower pot for two months, carefully dig up
one of them and inspect it for any signs of rooting. If there are no roots visible,
replant the cutting, close the bag, and set it back in the window. Hold summer cuttings until spring, winter cuttings until early summer. Then inspect them again, about
once a month during the growing season until the cutting roots appear, or turn black
or brown, indicating death.

After-rooting care. Follow these steps after the roots have appeared:

(1) Place the newly rooted cutting in a coldframe for one winter before transplanting it to its permanent bed.

(2) Just before transferring the cutting to the coldframe, open the plastic bag for an
hour or two each day, to prepare the cutting for open weather. Then, after a week,
remove the plant to the coldframe.

(3) If the cutting roots in spring or early summer, transplant it immediately from
the pot to an open coldframe. In the fall, cover the coldframe with plastic sheeting.

(4) If the cutting roots in late summer or fall, transplant it immediately from the pot
to a closed coldframe. You can also move the entire pot and cuttings to the coldframe
and transplant in the spring; set the pot deeply into the soil with its rim even with the
surface and fill in around the pot, pressing the soil firmly in place.

(5) In the spring, move the cutting to a nursery bed.

(6) Shade it and water it frequently during the first season. Most plants do not need
shading or special watering after the first crucial year.

(7) After it grows 12 to 24 inches tall, transplant the new tree or shrub from the
nursery bed to its permanent location in the garden.

A coldframe is a boxlike affair in which plants, seedlings, and cuttings can be grown while protected from outside weather conditions. Built with a back 9 to 12 inches higher than the front (right), a coldframe faces south so window sashes, shown leaning against back, will face into the sun.

LAYERING. When a branch of a plant is wounded and the wound is covered with soil or sphagnum moss, the branch will strike roots if it is still attached to the parent. It can then be cut off later and set out a as a new plant. This process of propagation is called layering.

Layering is usually done best in spring or late summer, when rooting is most vigorous in the coolish weather.

Simple layering. For a branch that sweeps low and touches the ground in its normal growing position, it is easy to wound a part, bury it, and wait for it to take root. This method of propagation is called simple layering.

Layering, incidentally, is a slow process; a spring-layered branch will form roots the following spring; a fall-layered branch will form roots the *second* spring.

Materials.
(1) Leaf mold or peat moss and sand.
(2) Rooting stimulant.
(3) Wooden peg or wire wicket for holding down branch.
(4) Mulch.

How to make a simple layering. Follow these easy steps:

(1) Prepare the soil in which the plant grows by working in leaf mold or peat moss and sand to enrich it.

(2) About 12 inches from the tip of the branch to be layered make a slanting cut 2 inches long on the upper side.

(3) Dust the cut with rooting stimulant.

(4) Pin the branch—now called the "layer"—down to the soil between the trunk of the shrub and the cut by means of a wooden peg or wire wicket, or the weight of a stone.

(5) Bend the tip of the branch upright, twisting it one-half a turn to open the cut.

(6) Place another peg or wicket directly over the branch at the cut to hold it there.

(7) Cover the layered branch with several inches of the leaf mold or peat moss and sand soil. Pile a mound of dirt 3 or 4 inches deep around the stem and pack it in solidly.

(8) Mulch the soil with straw and/or leaves. Water the branch frequently.

(9) When the layer has formed roots, whether the following spring, or the subsequent one, cut the rooted branch free.

(10) Leave the new plant in place for two or three weeks after severing it. Then transplant it to its new bed. Tend it there for at least a year.

Air layering. A variation of the practice of simple layering is to wound a branch that does not touch the ground, and wrap the wound with moistened sphagnum grass. This method is called "air layering."

Materials. Kits containing materials necessary for air layering are available at garden supply stores. If you do not buy a kit, you will need these materials:

(1) A sharp knife.

(2) Rooting stimulant.

(3) Sphagnum moss.

(4) A polyethylene plastic sheet.

(5) Plastic electrical tape.

How to make an air layering. Young branches one year old are ideal for air layering; older branches will take longer to root.

Branches layered in the spring should root by the following spring; branches layered in the fall should root by the second spring.

(1) Choose the "layer" portion of a branch and make it 12 to 18 inches from its tip. Remove any leaves within 6 inches of the point where the layer itself begins.

(2) Make a shallow, slanting cut about 2 inches long in the branch.

(3) Dust rooting stimulant into the cut and keep the cut open with a small splinter of wood inserted.

(4) Dampen a fist-sized ball of sphagnum moss and squeeze it as tightly as you can to remove all water.

(5) Cover the wound with the sphagnum moss.

(6) Wrap a 9 by 10 inch sheet of polyethylene plastic completely around the ball of moss; let the ends overlap.

(7) Twist both ends of the plastic tightly around the branch and fasten them securely with electrical tape.

(8) Do not let rain water seep into the package. If it appears at the ends, punch a small hole in the plastic to let the water out. Then seal again.

(9) Leave the air layer undisturbed for one growing season.

(10) After the roots have formed, remove the plastic wrapping and cut the branch below the roots.

(11) Set the plant in its new bed. Tend it carefully for at least a year.

After-layering care. Roots formed by layering are extremely small in relation to the branch. The leaves of the branch are liable to lose more water by transpiration than the small roots can pick up. You can control this loss by pruning all the side branches as soon as the layered branch is planted. Cut off at least one-third of each side branch.

Shade the new plants with screens made out of fencing, lath, reed matting, or burlap attached to wood. At the end of the first season, remove the screens. By that time the roots should be large enough to absorb enough water to live.

GRAFTS. A graft is the growing together of two different plants. The top of a graft (which includes the branches) is called the *scion,* and the bottom of the plant (which includes the roots and the bottom trunk) is called the *stock* or *rootstock.* To be successful, both scion and rootstock should be plants closely related to one another.

For the two halves to unite, the growing tissue of both scion and rootstock must be in close contact. Called the "cambium," the growing tissue is a soft layer of cells between the bark and the wood.

Horticulturists use many types of grafts to propagate trees and shrubs. The most commonly used types in the suburban garden are the bud graft and the cleft graft.

Five steps show how to accomplish a bud graft. A. Cut bud sticks from the plant, ¼″ from the bud. B. Cut T-shaped incision in bark of stock. C. Raise bark along both sides of cut. D. Insert the bud in the cut. E. Bind the graft with a rubber band to prevent drying.

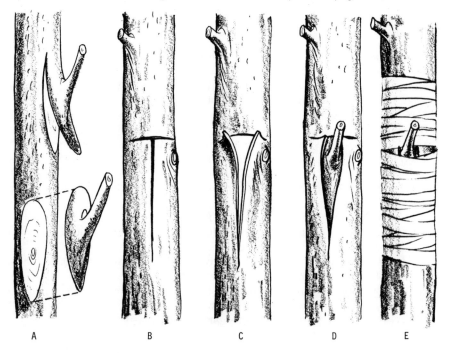

A   B   C   D   E

Bud graft. A bud graft can be made anytime during the growing season when the bark of the rootstock peels easily from the wood and the dormant buds are available. The bud is simply cut from one growing plant and inserted in a slit cut in a second plant.

Materials.

(1) Knife.

(2) Rubber band or plastic sheeting to hold bud in.

How to make a bud graft. For a rootstock, use a seedling or a rooted cutting. A good size for a rootstock is $\frac{3}{16}$ to $\frac{3}{8}$ inch in diameter, or about the thickness of a pencil.

(1) When the bud is plump but dormant, cut the bud stick from the desired plant, about $\frac{1}{4}$ inch from the bud. The piece of leaf stem that is left will protect the bud and can be used as a handle to hold the bud while working.

(2) Make a T-shaped cut in the bark of the rootstock, beginning the stem of the T near the ground and cutting upward about 1 inch. Make the horizontal cut at the top of the vertical. Extend the crosscut about one-third of the way around the rootstock. Cut only through the bark, not into the wood. With the point of the knife, lift the bark along both sides of the vertical cut for room to insert the bud.

(3) Starting about $\frac{1}{4}$ inch below the bud, cut into the scion only deep enough to take a thin sliver of wood with the bud. After the knife blade passes the bud, angle the cut upward and outward to remove the bud with a shield of bark about $\frac{3}{4}$ of an inch long.

(4) Insert the lower part of the bud shield into the rootstock T-cut. Push the T flaps down so the cut surface of the shield is flat against the wood of the rootstock. The bud shield should be completely enclosed in the T-cut. If part of the shield protrudes from the top of the T, cut it off.

(5) Wrap the cut with a piece of rubber band or a narrow strip of plastic sheeting. Make three or four turns below the bud and again above the bud. Do not cover the bud with wrapping.

(6) In three to five weeks, cut the wrapping away. By now, the bud should be united with the rootstock. It will usually remain dormant until the next season.

(7) In the early spring, cut off the top of the rootstock at a point about $\frac{1}{2}$ inch above the bud. This will force the bud to sprout. All growth from the bud up will be similar to the bud-source scion plant.

Cleft graft. The advantage of the cleft graft over the bud graft is that a large new plant can be propagated in a short time and that several varieties of a plant can be grown on the same main stem.

A cleft graft should be made while rootstock and scion are dormant; late winter is a good time.

Materials.

(1) Sharp knife or chisel.

(2) Saw or pruning shears.

(3) Grafting wax or tree-coating compound.

(4) Polyethylene (plastic) bag.

Grafting wax or tree-coating compound can be secured at any garden supply store.

How to make a cleft graft. Choose the scion wood from last year's growth to begin with. Then:

(1) Cut two scion stalks, each with three buds, for each rootstock. Cut the scions 1 inch below the lowest bud.

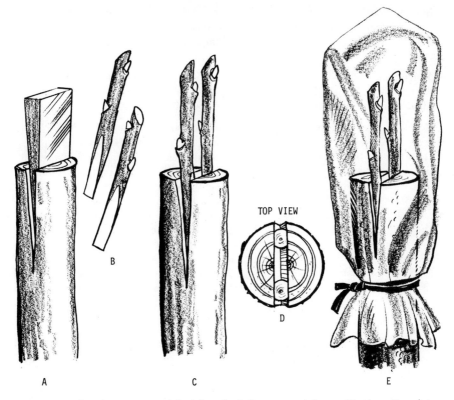

Four steps show how to accomplish cleft graft. *A.* Prepare stock for grafting by cutting slot across top and inserting wedge in slot. *B.* Prepare two wedge-shaped scions from each split stock. *C.* Insert scions in the stock so that cambium layers, where cells form, touch. Top view (*D*) shows how graft looks from above. *E.* Cover graft with plastic freezer bag.

(2) Square off the rootstock at the point you want to make the graft.

(3) Split the end of the rootstock with a broad chisel or knife about 2 or 3 inches down. Slip in a wedge to open up the split.

(4) Trim the butt of each scion branch to the shape of a wedge, starting the cuts at each side of the lowest bud, and making the wood on the bud side thicker than the opposite.

(5) Insert the scion in the split rootstock, with the lowest bud to the outside. Set the scion in at a slight angle so that the cambium layers of the rootstock and scion are definitely in contact. This is where the growth occurs.

(6) Remove the wedge from the rootstock.

(7) Coat all cut surfaces with grafting wax or tree-coating compound. Or tie a polyethylene bag around the graft, shading it from direct sunlight; leave the bag on until new growth fills the bag in the late spring, then remove it and cover all surfaces with tree-coating compound.

(8) Inspect the scions at the end of the growing season, and cut off the weaker of the two. Coat the stub with tree-coating compound.

HOW TO   HOW NOT TO

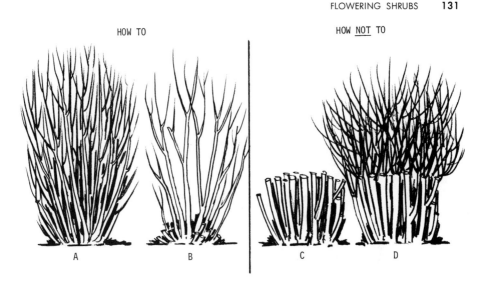

A   B   C   D

Well-pruned shrub should retain natural shape and habit of growth. To prune shrub correctly, remove some of old mature stems and dead or damaged canes down to ground. Drawings A and B show a shrub before and after pruning. Whacking off top of shrub as in C will cause top-heavy business (D) bushiness that destroys plant's natural shape and beauty.

PRUNING A FLOWERING SHRUB. There are two different kinds of flowering shrubs—those that bloom in the early spring, and those that bloom late in the summer. For those shrubs that bloom in the early spring, prune them only *after* the blossoms drop off. For those shrubs that bloom late in the summer, prune them in the early spring so that the new wood will stimulate flowering.

Spring-flowering shrubs include: azalea (*Rhododendron*), redbud (*Cercis*), dogwood (*Cornus*), bush honeysuckle (*Diervillea*), mountain laurel (*Kalmia*), kerria, leucothoe, mockorange (*Philadelphus*), andromeda (*Pieris*), rhododendron, jetbread (*Rhodotypos*), bridlewreath (*Spiraea*), lilac (*Syringa*), and snowball (*Viburnum*).

Late-flowering shrubs include: butterfly bush (*Buddleia*), sweet pepperbush (*Clethra alnifolia*), bluebeard (*Caryopteris*), rose of sharon (*Hibiscus syriacus*), hydrangea, and chaste-tree *(Vitex)*. With buddleia, carytopteris, vitex and their derivatives, you can cut them back to the ground each season without harm.

Most shrubs look best if they are allowed to grow naturally rather than being shaped into grotesque forms. Pruning of a shrub calls for removal of surplus parts without ruining its natural shape. Shearing is the clipping back of twig ends to promote a dense growth.

Shrubs that grow out from the base—forsythia, bush honeysuckles, and spireas, for instance—are best pruned by cutting away the old wood three or four years old close to the ground to allow the new shoots or canes to come in.

Shrubs that flower best at the tops of mature growth—lilacs for instance—are best pruned by cutting off suckers and new shoots at the bottom of the bush. It is sometimes difficult to differentiate between these two types of shrubs, but a little study will help.

As soon as lilac bloom dies, nip off seeds, being careful not to injure closest pair of leafy branches or they will not furnish blooms the following year.

To renew old lilac bush, cut out oldest stems — those dark in drawing — as close to soil level as possible. Use keyhole or other small pruning saw and avoid injury to bark of remaining stems.

In staking flowering shrubs, it is necessary to secure them with delicate bonds. Never use wire; it breaks the stem. Do not use string; it is unsightly and will rot in the garden. Use plastic strips or wire-covered green paper strips. When staking, tie a knot in the strip between the stake and the stem (A). Do not tie the stem and stake too closely (B).

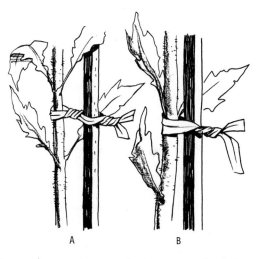

A   B

PRUNING FOR SHAPE. There are two main ways to prune back a tree or shrub: by thinning out or by heading back.

Thinning out means to remove some selected small and/or large branches, cutting them back to the point where they join side branches or to the point where they join the main trunk. By working this way, you end up with fewer cuts and leave fewer ugly stubs. Because you cut back only to the main branches and trunk, you will leave the remaining branches exactly as long as they were, retaining the proper silhouette and natural shape of the tree.

Heading back means to cut *every* branch back to a bud or to a side branch. The purpose of this procedure is to increase the bushiness of a plant; thinning out, as described above, opens up the plant to a larger size. The final silhouette and shape of a tree headed back will be smaller and thicker than when pruning was started. When heading back, retain the natural look of the plant by carefully shaping it with each cut you make. Do not let yourself whack at the branches hit-or-miss, or the result will be disastrous.

BEFORE   THINNING   HEADING BACK
A   B   C

These drawings show the difference between thinning and heading back a tree or shrub. A is a tree that needs thinning. B shows proper method of thinning by taking out whole branches close to main stalk. C shows proper way to head back plant by cutting back not only to the stalk in some instances but by clipping off ends, too.

9 | Hedges

A HEDGE IS A LINE OF SHRUBS or trees arranged to form a living fence. By spending a little money wisely, you can provide a living fence for your property for any number of valid reasons.

Because a hedge is a living thing, it is not quite so easy to take down as a fence. For that reason, always plan a hedge for permanence, visualizing exactly how big the hedge will be when fully grown, and how much maintenance it will require.

HEDGES WITH A PURPOSE. A low, trimmed hedge can be used to mark property lines inconspicuously but firmly. Compact plants make the best unclipped hedges, but they must be spaced closely together for the effect of denseness. Be sure to place a property-line hedge so that at maturity it will be growing entirely on your side of the line; otherwise, your neighbor will be within his rights to cut back any part that hangs over his ground.

Tough "keep-out" hedges can be grown of thonged shrubs, like barberry or hardy orange, either of which will discourage trespassing.

High, thick-textured hedges can be grown to screen out unsightly objects, like sprawling dumps on vacant lots, enormous utility tanks, or even ugly structures nearby.

Graceful, formal hedges can be used to enhance a house's architecture, particularly if the house itself has a formal outer aspect—like a Georgian, or a Colonial.

Hedges of all shapes and sizes can be used to provide lines in the general landscape design, if such lines are needed to complement or articulate certain aspects of the site.

Textured hedge settings can be used to show off small garden plots of annuals and perennials.

Thickly growing hedges can be used judiciously to blot out heavy traffic noises from a well-traveled street. They can also be used to filter out dust and dirt that might blow up from an unpaved road.

Small hedges, called edgings (explored later in this same chapter), can be used to act as borders to walkways, driveways, and the sidewalk.

Good thick hedges can even be used to protect lawns from excess traffic, flowers from being picked, and vegetable gardens from being vandalized.

High hedges can be used to screen out the sun or the wind.

HEDGE SHAPES. There are almost as many different hedge shapes possible as there are plants grown. However, a few trims work best for almost all hedge plants.

A flat-top hedge is the easiest to keep orderly, but in snowy and icy climates, the top may be damaged by accumulations of ice. A curved-top hedge can be more successful in northerly climes; trim it to slope down and outward at the sides.

As for the sides, the only suitable shape for a hedge is one that has the sides tapering outward toward the bottom. This shape will provide the bottom leaves with some sunlight and air. Otherwise, these lower sections will die, leaving a naked trunk to spoil the base of the hedge.

Classically sculptured hedge can be used to set off a walkway from a planting of trees as in this large city scene. Note ground cover under trees, blending in with the hedge and walk.

When you buy hedge plants, you generally will find illustrations and instructions for their proper trimming on the packages.

HEDGE SIZES. Unclipped, informal hedge plants tend naturally to grow to a certain height. It is most important to consider the height you want before you select an informal plant. You may be able to trim it back a few inches, but do not keep a plant that wants to grow 10 feet high back at four or five.

In many cases hedge plants will reach a specific height if allowed to grow unclipped. However, they can be maintained at any size in between minimum clipping height and maturity by constant trimming.

The distance between each plant in a hedge can be determined by instructions on the package in which the plants come; you can always squeeze plants together for a denser hedge, or pull them apart for a loose growth.

Generally speaking, you can space hedge plants anywhere from 18 to 36 inches apart; usually you will not be planting anything closer than 18 inches unless it be a dwarf type.

Poor man's hedge acts as border to pyramidal arborvitae (center), cypress (left), and hardy rubbertree (right). Hedge is made up of native deciduous specimens planted closely together — beech, birch, dogwood, maple, oaks, ash — and trimmed in a tight hedge shape.

135

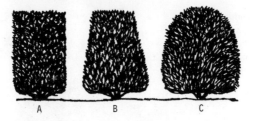

Hedge tops can be cut both rounded or flat. Flat top is easiest to keep orderly with trimming, but can be damaged by large accumulations of snow and ice. Trim shapes A and B serve for temperate zones, but C is the best for year-round service in north.

Drawings show how *not* to shape a hedge. The hedge top wider than bottom (A) will prevent sun from reaching lower branches, stifling them. Lower branches are also stunted in B and C.

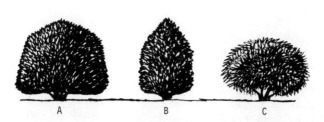

These three shapes are best for special types of evergreens. Use A for hemlock, B for yew, and C for trimming mugho pine.

American arborvitae can be planted together in compact line and trimmed into hedge shape as shown here.

KINDS OF HEDGE PLANTS. Two types of evergreens—broad-leaved and narrow-leaved—are excellent choices for hedge projects because they are easily trained to assume the shape you want.

Broad-leaved evergreens can be trimmed firmly and severely without being hurt; they are slow-growing plants that branch and bush out readily under proper pruning. They include these genuses: azeleas; boxwoods; rhododendrons; holly (English and Japanese); leucothoë; pieris; mountain laurel; cotoneaster; Daphne; euonymous; and barberry.

Some of the above have flowers, some have berries, and some present a solid mass of foliage only. All make excellent hedge prospects.

Narrow-leaved evergreens include two types: those plants that can be used for hedges and foundation plants; and those that grow separately and can be used only for individual specimens.

Hedge and foundation types include: arborvitae; yews; Mugho pine; dwarf Alberta spruce; Japanese black pine; creeping juniper; Greek juniper; and false cypress.

Specimen types, good also for high windbreaks, include: hemlock; white pine; Scotch pine; Colorado blue spruce; white spruce; Norway spruce; white cedar; white fir; Nikko fir; blue Atlantic cedar; cryptomeria, and Douglas fir.

THREE FORMAL CLIPPED HEDGE PLANTS. Amur privet (*Ligustrum amurense*). Most extensively cultivated hedge plant in existence. Tolerates extreme cold well; can be grown almost anywhere in the United States. Tiny white flowers in late spring and small black berries in early fall. Privets grow to 15 feet or so, but can be limited by trimming. [Zone 3]

Common Lantana (*Lantana camara*). Will take tight pruning and bloom continually until first frost. Thrives in dry soil. Clusters of red and yellow flowers, followed by small blueblack fruits. From 4' to 10' and grows almost everywhere in the South. [Zone 8]

Brush-cherry Eugenia (*Eugenia paniculata*). Forms a dense, purplish green hedge under regular pruning. Rose-purple fruits edible, ripe throughout the year. Widely used in California and Florida. Grows to 40'. [Zone 9]

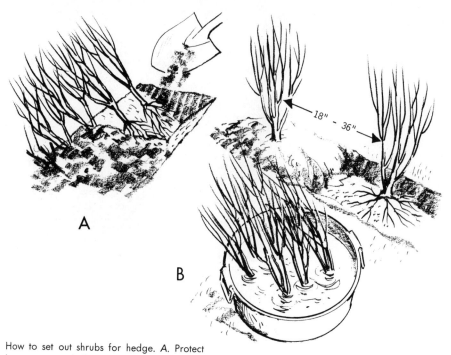

How to set out shrubs for hedge. *A*. Protect bare roots until they are in ground. *B*. Set shrub plants 18 to 36 inches apart, depending on type of hedge and type of shrub. *C*. Set the hedge plant in at the same height it originally grew. *D*. Spread five roots out so they head into soil around the hole, then add food and water. *E*. Form a basin to catch water for irrigation; cover all with good mulch.

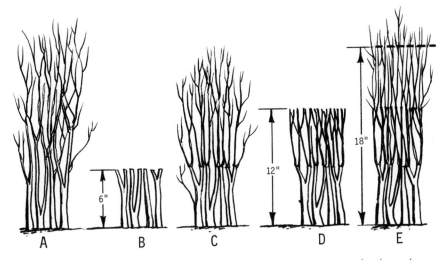

How to start a privet hedge. *A.* First set out plants close together. *B.* Immediately cut them down to 6 inches high. *C.* Allow hedge to grow the first season with no summer pruning. *D.* At end of first growing season, cut back to 12 inches. *E.* Growth during second season may be cut back to 18 inches during summer.

THREE LOW-EDGING HEDGES Globe arborvitae *(Thuja occidentalis globosa).* Will grow in almost all the northern states; bright, shiny green color. Good low edging hedge when individual shrubs are planted close together. Prune to stimulate lateral spread. [Zone 2]

Euonymous *(Euonymus japonicus mocrophylla).* Popular in the South, where it grows in dry soil and sandy places. Grows upright, with dainty, glistening thick foliage. Can be kept clipped to a small size. [Zone 7]

True Dwarf Box *(Buxus sempervirens suffruticosa).* Widely grown here since colonial times. Perfect for edging flower beds or walls. Can be sheared back severely, since it sprouts quickly from old wood. Can be used for an informal, untrimmed hedge. Grows to about 3'. [Zone 5]

THREE TALL BACKGROUND HEDGE PLANTS. Cockspur thorn *(Crataegus crus-galli).* Most popular of the native American hawthorns. Forms a thick hedge barrier, armed with thorns and growing with horizontal branching. White flowers, and bright red fruits that come and stay all winter. Grows in the northern states. [Zone 4]

Gossamer Sydney acacia *(Acacia longifolia).* Warm-climate tree. Can be trained into a dense high hedge, with plants spaced 4 to 5 feet apart; it will grow 20 feet high. Bright gold flower spikes 2½ inches long that appear in February and March. [Zone 10]

Yaupon *(Ilex vomitoria).* Holly plant that grows in the South and Southwest. Can be easily sheared into hedge form, and grows to 24' in height. Fruits are red, small, borne singly or in 3's. Most heavily fruited of the hollies, and most drought-resistant. [Zone 7]

THREE BORDER HEDGE PLANTS. Dwarf Cranberrybush *(Viburnum opulus).* Particularly suited to edgings and grows in wet or heavy clay soil. Let it grow informally, for it will not get over 3' high. Dense shrub; bright red fruits and red foliage in the fall. Grows best in the central-east and northern states. [Zone 3]

Dwarf true myrtle *(Myrtus communis nana).* Grown only in the warmest spots of the United States. Aromatic evergreen leaves; small creamy-white flowers in summer. Blue-black berries in fall. Can be sheared and easily shaped to any form desirable. [Zone 8-9]

Dwarf pomegranate *(Punica granatum).* Popular garden shrub in the South, coast to coast. Flowers scarlet and over 1 inch wide. Blooms throughout May and June; Red fruit 2½ inches through.

THREE INFORMAL HEDGE PLANTS. Rugosa rose *(Rosa rugosa).* Grows throughout the northern states. Hardy, resistant to insects, disease, poor soil and cold weather. Bright pink flowers and brick-red "tomato" fruits. As untrimmed hedge, grows to about 4', and will blossom even if clipped periodically. [Zone 2]

Oleander *(Nerium oleander).* Needs little attention and grows well in a garden. Tolerant to heat and drought; White, yellow, red or purple flowers. Handsome informal hedge plant, but grows mostly in the warmer parts of the country. [Zone 7-8]

Duranta *(Duranta plumieri).* Also known as the skyflower because flowers soft blue. Will grow to 18', and sometimes has spiny stems that make it a good barrier hedge. Bright-yellow berried through the winter. Also called the golden dewdrop, because its fruits are borne in golden-yellow clusters like currants. [Zone 10]

LIST OF GOOD HEDGE PLANTS. The following list of plants for hedges has been arranged for easy selection according to the height of plant desired – either trimmed or natural.

To find a formal plant for a 4-foot clipped hedge, run down the column headed MINIMUM CLIPPED HEIGHT until you come to the figure 4. Every plant appearing alongside a figure 4 can be trimmed back to 4 feet. So can all species with the figure 3, or 2, or 1 in the MINIMUM CLIPPED HEIGHT column, provided the figure in ULTIMATE NATURAL HEIGHT column is 4 or more.

To find an informal hedge plant that will grow to a 4-foot height without trimming, run your finger down the second column – ULTIMATE NATURAL HEIGHT – and select any of the plants listed. Hardiness zone is listed too, along with E for evergreen and D for deciduous.

PRUNING A FORMAL HEDGE. The privet hedge is the most common kind of formal hedge in use today. It requires special treatment.

When it is first set out, cut each plant back to 6 inches above the ground. At the end of the first growing season, cut each back to 12 inches, or lower. Cut straight across the top of the plant, maintaining it flat. During the second growing season, but back the top growth halfway several times during the summer. Then, at the end of the second growing season, cut each plant back to 18 inches.

Be sure that you cut the top of the hedge flat across. Do not allow the width of the top of the plant to exceed the width of the bottom. Taper the plant out as you work down from the top. Bottom branches will die out if deprived of sunlight.

Other hedge plants do not need to be clipped quite so often as the privet. For instance, you should trim the privet about once a month in fast-growing seasons, but

Battery-operated hedge trimmers are best for a formal yew hedge. Sweep the blades straight across the top for an even cut, and straight along the sides at the desired angle. Electric trimmers work well with needle- and broad-leaved evergreen trees.

the slow-growing hemlock about once or twice a season. Clip any newly planted hedge back to 6 inches—like the privet.

To encourage branching in hedges, clip back heavily each year before the new growth starts, until the hedge achieves the proper height you want.

Evergreens that are not used as hedge plants should be handled a little more delicately. Trim coniferous plants only if you want a formal shape. Never try to cut a conifer back too hard. Prune evergreen hedge plants from May through July, removing only short lengths from the branches. In this way you can control the shape much more easily and protect the plants.

If you wish to limit the hedge and/or plant to one specific size, cut off the leader and be sure to go over the side branches too. (There is more detailed information on Pruning Evergreens in Chapter 7.)

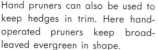

Hand pruners can also be used to keep hedges in trim. Here hand-operated pruners keep broad-leaved evergreen in shape.

Pachysandra, used as edging plant, divides grass lawn in foreground from the garden area. Garden includes high-domed yew, several spreading yew alongside, gladiolas, and iris. Ground cover can double as edging plant.

Variety of edging plants and flowers in conjunction with rocks divides a lawn from the house. Yews, wide-leaved evergreen, fern, and flowers are used in this border planting.

Pachysandra separates this rock wall and its brick border along the curving driveway. Large and small hemlocks (left), rising out of the edging of azaleas, add natural overtones to a man-made road.

EDGING PLANTS. The edging plant—actually a mini-hedge—is used to enhance the border of a walkway, a garden plot, a driveway, the sidewalk, or a formal setting of some kind. Plants used in edgings are usually low, compact, and neat. Ideally, they are plants that can be trimmed easily and continually.

Select your edging plants to produce the maximum foliage through the entire growing season. The evergreen is an excellent choice for such a plant; but so are many deciduous plants.

The shape of the edging plant is the determining factor in its selection. You may like a low, clipped hedge. Or you may like a long string of round plants that sit together like beads on a string. Or you may have some other idea in mind, like edging under hedge or background planting.

Here is a small list of much-used edging plants. There are others, of course. This is simply a sampler:

PRUNING HEDGES. The purpose of pruning hedges and ornamental trees and shrubs is four-fold: to keep them shapely, to prevent future damage, to promote new growth, and to rejuvenate aging plants.

Most ornamental trees need only moderate pruning, just enough to keep them growing in the most pleasant shape possible. However, when it can be seen that damage will result from an overladen branch, or from a collision with a fence, pruning can keep the plant healthy.

As you cut out portions of the dormant growth in any tree or shrub, you make it possible for the new growths in the plant to get a greater share of the food stored in the roots. And by getting rid of dead branches, you help the plant to come back from an almost dormant condition.

A formal hedge, of course, requires an almost entirely different kind of treatment than a flowering shrub.

Edging plants like English ivy and a variety of broad-leaved evergreen foundation plants are used to cover the sterile ground between the sidewalk and building.

INSTANT HEIGHT LOCATOR FOR HEDGE PLANTS

MINIMUM CLIPPED HEIGHT	MINIMUM CLIPPED HEIGHT	COMMON NAME	LATIN NAME	EVERGREEN OR DECIDUOUS	ZONE
1'	4'	Privet honeysuckle	(Lonicera pileata)	E	5
1½'	2'	Magellan barberry	(Berberis buxifolia nana)	E	5
2'	4'	Convex Japanese holly	(Ilex crenata convexa)	E	6
2'	4'	Regel privet	(Ligustrum obtusifolium regelianum)	D	3
2'	5'	Black chokecherry	(Aronia melanocarpa)	D	4
2'	6'	Box honeysuckle	(Lonicera nitida)	E	7
	3'	Bumalda spirea	(Spiraea bumalda)	D	5
	3'	Dwarf cranberry bush	(Viburnum opulus nanum)	D	3
	3'	Scotch rose	(Rosa spinosissima)	D	4
	3'	Kelsey dwarf dogwood	(Cornus sericea kelseyi)	D	2
3'	4'	Cushion Japanese yew	(Taxus cuspidata densa)	E	4
3'	12'	European privet	(Ligustrum vulgare)	D	4
	4'	Bush cinquefoil	(Potentilla fruticosa)	D	2
	4'	Garland spirea	(Spiraea arguta)	D	4
	4'	Slender deutzia	(Deutzia gracilis)	D	4
4'	8'	Rosemary barberry	(Berberis stenophylla)	E	5
4'	9'	Bayberry	(Myrica pensylvanica)	D	2
4'	15'	Amur privet	(Ligustrum amurense)	D	3
	5'	Glossy abelia	(Abelia grandiflora)	D	5
	5'	Hills-of-snow	(Hydrangea arborescens)	D	4
5'	9'	Red chokeberry	(Aronia arbutifolia)	D	4
5'	15'	Japanese privet	(Ligustrum japonicum)	E	2
	6'	Sweetbrier	(Rosa eglanteria)	D	4
	6'	Winter honeysuckle	(Lonicera fragrantissima)	D	5
6'	10'	Cherry prinsepia	(Prinsepia sinensis)	D	4
6'	10'	Darwin barberry	(Berberis darwinii)	E	7
6'	10'	Dwarf white spruce	(Picea glauca conica)	E	2
6'	15'	Japanese yew	(Taxus cuspidata)	E	4
6'	20'	Hicks yew	(Taxus cuspidata hicksii)	E	4
6'	20'	Silver red cedar	(Juniperus virginiana glauca)	E	2
6'	25'	Glossy privet	(Ligustrum lucidum)	E	7
6'	30'	California bayberry	(Myrica californica)	D	7
6'	30'	Dahoon	(Ilex cassine)	E	7
	7'	Father Hugo's rose	(Rosa hugonis)	D	5
7'	10'	Pfitzer juniper	(Juniperus chinensis pfitzeriana)	E	4
7'	14'	Black haw	(Viburnum prunifolium)	D	3
	8'	Dwarf winged euonymus	(Euonymus alatus)	D	3
	8'	Sargent crab apple	(Malus sargentii)	D	4
8'	20'	Swedish juniper	(Juniperus communis suecica)	E	2

ULTIMATE NATURAL HEIGHT	ULTIMATE NATURAL HEIGHT	COMMON NAME	LATIN NAME	EVERGREEN OR DECIDUOUS	ZONE
8'	35'	American hornbeam	*(Carpinus caroliniana)*	D	2
	9'	Chinese holly	*(Ilex cornuta)*	E	7
	9'	Austrian brier	*(Rosa foetida)*	D	4
	9'	Tatarian honeysuckle	*(Lonicera tatarica)*	D	3
	15'	Columnar juniper	*(Juniperus chinensis pyramidalis)*	E	4
	15'	Peegee hydrangea	*(Hydrangea paniculata grandifloria)*	D	4
10'	35'	European hornbeam	*(Carpinus betulus)*	D	5
	20'	Amur maple	*(Acer ginnala)*	D	2
	22'	Cornelian cherry	*(Cornus mas)*	D	4
	30'	Washington thorn	*(Crataegus phaenopyrum)*	D	4

EDGING PLANTS

COMMON NAME	BOTANICAL NAME	HEIGHT	ZONE
Bugleweed/Carpet Bugle	*(Ajuga reptans)*	6"	4
Snapdragon	*(Antirrhinum majus)* dwarf vars.	6"	annual or perennial
Dwarf Magellan Barberry	*(Berberis buxifolia nana)*	18"	5
Japanese Barberry	*(Berberis thunbergii)*	7"	4
Dwarf Box	*(Buxus sempervirens suffruticosa)*	1–3"	5–6
Dwarf Eared Coreopsis	*(Coreopsis auriculata nana)*	6"	4
Blue Fescue	*(Festuca ovina glauca)*	12"	4
Crested Iris	*(Iris cristata)*	3"–4"	3
True Lavender	*(Lavandula officinalis)* dwarf vars.	12"	5
Edging Lobelia	*(Lobelia erinus)*	4"–12"	annual
Japanese Spurge	*(Pachysandra terminalis)*	8"	5
Moss Pink	*(Phlox subulata)*	6"	2–3
Sedum	*(Sedum species)*	2"–3'	2–3
Nasturtium	*(Tropaeolum)* dwarf vars.	10"	annual
Tufted Pansy	*(Viola cornuta)*	6"	2–3
Johnny-jump-up	*(Viola tricolor)*	6"–12"	4

10 | Accents

Foundation plants are those used around the walls of a house and planted at ground level in order to give added texture to an exterior or to accentuate or supplement the surface itself with form and shape.

A foundation plant should not be too tall, especially if it is to grow in front of a window. A tall shrub or tree should be reserved for use along the portion of a wall where there are no windows at all, or at a place near the corner of the building where it can help the house blend in with the surrounding foliage and lawn.

Vines and ground covers blend well with foundation plants, and have special uses that will be discussed at the end of this chapter.

The evergreen has a primary advantage as a foundation plant: it remains green throughout the year, and it may even bear blossoms. Both needle-leaved and broad-leaved evergreens are excellent next to the house because they give a permanent variance of texture to contrast with the flat machine-made lines of the house.

It is a wise idea when planning foundation plants to keep away as much as possible from formal shapes. Nothing is deadlier than a formal house surrounded by formal foundation plants and led to by a formal edged walk. That kind of rigidity gives the house an artificial look—exactly what you are striving to avoid.

Before discussing how to use foundation plants, let's take a look at certain types: broad-leaved evergreens; ground covers; and vines.

THE BROAD-LEAVED EVERGREEN. This attractive conifer is a formidable plant to use in foundation settings. Not only does it keep its shape and texture throughout the year, but it presents a mood and tone quite different from the needle-leaved evergreen discussed in Chapter 6.

In modern landscaping, the broad-leaved evergreen has come into its own as a most serviceable plant. Its rough texture helps blend man-made structural materials with ground cover, vines, grass and rock forms. Because it is natural, it blends in well not only with other rough textures, but also with smooth and slick textures.

Combined with ground cover, the broad-leaved evergreen as foundation and accent plant is ideally suited to combat the artificiality of structural lines.

What follows is only a partial list of broad-leaved evergreens, but it includes the workhorses of the species.

Andromeda (*Pieris japonica*). This is about the best broad-leaved evergreen for ornamental planting in the North. It is 9 feet tall, with lustrous, deep green leaves, up to $3\frac{1}{2}$ inches long. Drooping flower clusters 5 inches long and dense foliage combine to make this an excellent ornamental. Flowers appear about mid-April; young foliage is often rich bronze in the spring, turning green as it matures. Will grow in the shade; but some sunshine is needed to force it into a good display of flowers.

Azalea (*Rhododendron*). Botanically, the azalea is classified as a rhododendron, and, like the rhododendron, the azalea does well in a cool climate with plenty of moisture in the atmosphere. Both do well in acid soil and moist earth. Some azaleas are

Yew trimmed in the classic box shape serves as border accents to this small porch. The beauty of the yew is that it grows in acid soil and retains its shape if trimmed assiduously.

Rhododendrons and pachysandra edge grass are used here as a border along a driveway under Norway spruce (left) and horse chestnut.

evergreen, but most are deciduous. The texture of their broad leaves and the richness of their flowers make them one of the best of all low-growing, broad-leaved evergreen plants.

Barberry (*Berberis*). The shrub has bright yellow flowers, and red, yellow, blue, or black fruits. The barberry generally is subject to black stem rust disease; be sure to get a species immune or resistant to it.

Boxwood (*Buxus sempervirens*). Two species, *Buxus sempervirens* and *Buxus microphylla,* are used for ornamental planting in the United States. Littleleaf box *(Buxus microphylla)* is hardier and lower-growing than common box *(Buxus sempervirens)*. Boxwood grows in the Eastern and Southern United States. It prefers limestone soil, but will do well also in acid soils. Boxwood can be trimmed severely, and kept in classic lines, or let grow wild.

Cotoneaster (*Cotoneaster microphylla*). The small evergreen leaves of the cotoneaster, as well as its scarlet berries in fall, make it a fine border or foundation specimen. It can be used alongside a house or in a rock garden.

Holly (*Ilex*). There are at least 21 species of native American holly, 120 Oriental, and 200 English. Some holly plants are hardy enough for the extreme North; others require warmer regions. Some produce yellow fruits; others red fruits. There are dwarf varieties for special purposes. Generally, holly can be used as a foundation plant; it is compatible with vines, ground covers, edgings, and flowers of all kinds.

Leucothoë (*Leucothoë fontanesiana*). Called drooping leucothoë, this is a native American evergreen in the South; semi-evergreen in the North. It has white, waxy flowers, like blueberries, in early June, on small racemes hanging down under gracefully arching stems. Its dark, lustrous evergreen leaves, up to 7 inches long, turn

Ground cover of pachysandra blends admirably into rising fountain of leucothoë near this house wall and chimney. Both act as a setting for flowering dogwood.

bronze in the fall and last all winter. It is best to keep leucothoë under 3 feet high. It grows well everwhere that rhododendrons do.

Mountain Laurel (*Kalmia latifolia*). A beautiful, flowering evergreen shrub native to Eastern North America. It has pink and white and even red flowers about mid-June. It likes acid soil. It is an evergreen member of the Heath Family. Mountain laurel gives good background texture to any landscaping.

Rhododendron (*Rhododendron*). The leather-leaved evergreen rhododendron is valued as a landscape plant wherever it can be grown. It prefers an acid soil not exposed to the hot summer sun. Good rhododendron soil should contain plenty of humus or decaying organic matter. It is a direct cousin of the azalea, and prefers much the same climate and soil conditions. Incidentally, both plants blend well with each other, affording a rough, tough texture.

NEEDLE-LEAVED EVERGREENS. Needle-leaved evergreens used in foundation and accent planting include arborvitae (*Thuja*), fir (*Abies*), juniper (*Juniperus*), Mugho dwarf pine *(Pinus)*, Pfitzer juniper *(Juniperus)*, spruce *(Picea)*, and yew *(Taxus)*, which have been covered in Chapter 6, Evergreens.

Deciduous shrubs used in foundation and accent planting include bridlewreath (*Spiraea*), butterfly bush (*Buddleia*), chaste-tree (*Vitex*), cherry-laurel (*Prunus*), deutzia, dogwood (*Cornus*), eunymous, flowering quince (*Chaenomeles*), forsythia, hawthorn (*Crataegus*), hibiscus, honeysuckle (*Lonicera*), hydrangea, magnolia, mockorange (*Philadelphius*), rose, snowball (*viburnum*), spicebush (*Calycanthus*), and weigela.

GROUND COVERS. A ground cover is a low-growing plant used to improve the appearance of any bare area, or to protect a slope from erosion. It has a more specialized use in conjunction with foundation plants, both to give texture to their background and to help blend the lawn grass in with the rough texture of the accent plants.

In modern landscaping, ground covers are used more and more as background and accent devices to draw the eye away from the formal lines of a structure, to help remove the structure from the foreground, and to give a harsh and pleasing carpet on which other rough-textured plants can grow.

Of course, a ground cover can also be used as a substitute for turf where grass will not grow or to cut down on the mowing area. A ground cover needs little maintenance and will form a dense and compact mat on the earth that will not vary from season to season.

However, unlike lawn turf, it must not be walked upon or played upon. It is, nevertheless, an excellent choice when weather and soil conditions preclude the use of lawn or other plantings.

The following list contains a number of ground covers used in certain adverse situations:

GROUND COVER SUBSTITUTES FOR GRASS. On some sites grass absolutely will not grow. Either the soil will not nurture growth, or the climate will not support turf.

In such a situation your best bet is to substitute a low-growing plant for grass. There are a number of plant species that will give an excellent ground cover simulating a rich turf grass and prevent soil erosion.

Heavily shaded areas, very steep banks where mowing and sowing is difficult, under or around hedges where you cannot cultivate: all these situations call for substitution.

Here are a number of the most popular:

Dichondra (*Dichondra repens*). In the desert sections of California and in other very dry Western areas, *Dichondra repens* can be used in place of grass. Related to

Rhododendron hedge acts as a background for a sisal hemp specimen in a metal pot. Hedge goes well with needle-leaved fir at left.

English ivy (right foreground) blends in with rhododendron and other broad-leaved evergreens to give a natural border to a pond next to a house.

Periwinkle, also called creeping myrtle, is one of the most adaptable of ground covers. It grows thick and makes a perfect texture for bare ground where grass doesn't grow easily. Plant produces blue blossoms in spring.

Although actually not ground cover at all, coleus, known popularly as "foliage plant," can grow in buckets or in edgings to bring blue, purple, and red colors to plain green backgrounds.

GROUND COVER FOR SHADY PLACES

COMMON NAME	BOTANICAL NAME	ZONE	HEIGHT	COLOR	BLOOMS
Ground Ivy	*(Nepeta nederacea)*	3	3″	Blue	May-Sept.
Lily of the valley	*(Convallana majalis)*	2	8″	White	Spring
Periwinkle	*(Vinca minor)*	4	6″	Blue	Summer
St. John's-wort	*(Hypericum calcycinum)*	6	1′	Yellow	Summer
Stonecrops	*(Sedum spurium)*	3–10	2–12″	Pink, white	July-Aug.

GROUND COVER FOR PARTIALLY SHADY PLACES

Bugleweed	*(Ajuga reptans)*	4	4–12″	Blue, white	Summer
Canby Pachistima	*(Paxistima canbyi)*	5	12″	White	Bronze in fall
Hall's Creeping Mahonia	*(Mahonia repens)*	5	10″	Yellow	Summer
Lily-turf	*(Liriope* species*)*	4–7	8–24″	White	July-Aug.
Thyme	*(Thymus* species*)*	3–4	1–8″	Rose to violet	Summer

GROUND COVER FOR SUNNY PLACES

Candytuft	*(Iberis sempervirens)*	3	12″	White	Spring
Creeping Polemonium	*(Polemonium reptans)*	2–3	24″	Blue to rose	Spring
Creeping Speedwell	*(Veronica repens)*	5	4–12″	Blue	July
Prostrate Broom	*(Cytisus decumbens)*	5	8″	White	May
Snow-in-summer	*(Cerastium tomentosum)*	2	3–6″	White	Spring

GROUND COVER FOR MOIST PLACES

Creeping Phlox	*(Phlox stolonifera)*	2–3	5–12″	Purple	Spring
Forget-me-not	*(Myosotis sylvatica)*	annual	9–24″	Blue	Summer
Leather Bergenia	*(Bergenia crassifolia)*	2–3	20″	Pink	Spring
Partridge-berry	*(Mitchella repens)*	3	2″	White	April
Swamp Dewberry	*(Rubus hispidus)*	3	prostrate	White	June

the morning glory; this perennial vine is grown for its profusion of half-inch roundish leaves rather than for its flowers. It spreads into a dense, creeping growth rapidly, and takes transplants easily. It grows wherever temperatures do not drop below 25 degrees Fahrenheit.

English Ivy (*Hedera helix*). This plant thrives in dense shade. It will grow happily under high shade trees, and under dense growths. However, it will *not* grow on terraced slopes that are hit by the sun.

Wintercreeper (*Euonymus radicans*). Wintercreeper has a beautiful dark-green foliage. It will thrive as English ivy does in dense shade that is not penetrated by sunlight at all. What is very good about wintercreeper is that, unlike ivy, it will grow on sunny slopes.

Periwinkle, Trailing Myrtle (*Vinca minor*). Provides glossy green foliage in shaded areas. It grows very well on steep banks that will not take grass because of erosion.

Japanese Spurge (*Pachysandra*). Good evergreen ground cover, Japanese spurge builds up a strong growth both in dense shade and on steep slopes. It even has a small flower that gives it added distinction.

Ponyfoot (*Dichondra carolinensis*). Also called lawnfoot, this plant can be used on spotty lawns because it spreads quickly and covers the ground with leaves and stems.

The covering is not as pleasing as real grass. Ponyfoot does not stand up well to traffic and does not winter well.

Pearlwort (*Sagina*). A mosslike plant, pearlwort will make a unique and beautiful lawn if you plant plugs of it about 6 inches apart. Water and roll it faithfully, weed and fertilize regularly, and the result is a lawn that does not require mowing. Pearlwort thrives on northern exposures in dense shade.

HOW TO USE VINES. A vine is any plant that trails along the ground or climbs by twining or by attaching to some means of support like a wire, a trellis, a tree trunk, or a wall.

There are three ways in which a vine can climb.

(1) By twining itself around a pole, plant, or other tree.

(2) By attaching tendrils or leaf stalks to a wire or branch.

(3) By attaching discs or footlike hold-fasts to a flat surface.

A vine that climbs by twining and a vine that climbs by attaching tendrils needs a trellis, a fence, or a wire support to cling to. A vine that climbs by attaching discs can go up any wall. Usually it prefers to climb a stone, brick, or plaster surface.

Trellises. Trellises can be made of laths or slats nailed together in a cross-hatch pattern, and then propped up to serve as independent supports.

A vine that shoots out tendrils or leaf stalks can always be led up a trellis made of chicken wire or wire mesh. Or it can be led up wire supports.

A vine that attaches hold-fasts to a wall can be trained to climb a brick surface, a plaster surface, or a concrete surface. It is not a wise idea to let such a vine climb up a

Trellis made of strips of latticework, attached to the side of a garage, provides support for a wisteria vine. A trellis can be attached to a structure or it stands on its own.

wooden surface; the vine must be completely removed before the surface can be repainted, and then the vine must be started all over again.

VINES FOR THE SUBURBAN GARDENER. Although the following three lists—of vines that twine cling by tendrils, and cling by hold-fasts—are not complete, they include most of the vines that are popular and suitable for use in the average small home garden.

VINES THAT CLIMB BY TWINING

COMMON NAME	BOTANICAL NAME	HARDINESS ZONE	FOLIAGE	SPECIAL PROBLEMS
Bittersweet	(Celastrus)	2–4	Deciduous	
Brazil Bougain-villea	(Bougainvillea spectabilis)	10	Evergreen	
Dutchman's Pipe	(Aristolochia durior)	4	Deciduous	
Honeysuckle	(Lonicera)	3–9	Deciduous	
Morning-glory	(Ipomoea purpurea)		Annual	
Star-jasmine	(Trachelosperumu)	7–9	Evergreen	
Wisteria	(Wisteria)	4–6	Deciduous	Can strangle itself with twining shoots. Prune in winter, shortening all shoots to 3 feet. Protect from rabbits with 3-foot-high wire-mesh screen around base.

VINES THAT CLIMB BY ATTACHING TENDRILS

Calabash Gourd	(Lagenaria siceraria)		Annual	
Carolina Jessamine	(Gelsemium semper-vierns)	7	Evergreen	
Clematis	(Clematis)	4–7	Deciduous	Climbs by leaf-stalks. May wilt. Look for break or cut; start over near base. Rabbits may sever tops.
Grape	(Vitis)	2–6	Deciduous	May wrap tendrils on tree branches. If double ring of swelling around tree branch, cut tendrils away and pull away grape plant.
Madeira-vine	(Boussingaultia baselloides)	9	Evergreen	
Nasturtium	(Tropaeolum majus)		Annual	
Sweet Pea	(Lathyrus odoratus)		Annual	

VINES THAT CLIMB BY ATTACHING HOLD-FASTS

Blood Trumpet-vine	(Phaedranthus buccinatorius)	9	Evergreen	
Climbing Hydrangea	(Hydrangea anomala petiolaris)	4	Deciduous	
Ivy	(Hedera)	5–7	Evergreen	Protect from rabbits with 3-foot high wire-mesh screen around base.

COMMON NAME	BOTANICAL NAME	HARDINESS ZONE	FOLIAGE	SPECIAL PROBLEMS
Orange-trumpet	(*Pyrostegia venusta*)	10	Evergreen	
Philodendron	(*Philodendron*)	10	Evergreen	
Virginia Creeper	(*Parthenocissus quinquefolia*)	3–8	Deciduous	
Wintercreeper	(*Euonymus fortunei varieties*)	5	Evergreen	Protect from rabbits with 3-foot high wire-mesh fence around base. Scale insects may attack.

HOW TO USE FOUNDATION PLANTS. Evergreens, both needle-leaved and broad-leaved, can be used with great success as foundation plants; so can many deciduous trees and shrubs; so can ground covers in conjunction with accent plants of all kinds; so, too, can various vines and climbing plants.

Mixing these together is a skill that can be acquired after careful study. It can also be acquired by the simple expedient of trial and error.

The following discussion on the use of foundation plants of all kinds is very broad and very brief, but will give you an idea of some of the problems you may encounter and their solutions.

Foundation shrubs. The size of the house dictates the size of the foundation plants used around it. Obviously you will be putting in smaller plants to decorate a one story house than you will be to decorate a three story house.

The smallest plants should go under windows or perhaps in front of larger plants if you use clumps at the corners for a desired effect. These small plants can be ground cover like myrtle, pachysandra, English ivy, or bugleweed, mixed in with some bulbs and low-growing perennials.

Slightly larger plants—still ground-cover species—can be dwarf juniper, pachistima, or box sandmyrtle.

Near the front entrance to the house, use slightly taller plantings. Shrubs on each side of the entryway, porch, or walk will frame the doorway in an interesting living texture. Such shrubs as yew, Japanese holly, small-leaved rhododendron, or andromeda might do the trick.

Be sure not to let these crowd each other, or push in to dominate the door or the effect of an entryway will be ruined. Select these plants with extreme care, paying particular attention to the size they will be at maturity and making sure that they will not be able to overpower the house and draw too much attention away from other specimens.

Foundation flowers. For extremely small but bright accents, plan to use some annual flowers along with some edging plants. Bulbs and perennials placed in together will add a great deal of color and impact. Select these according to your taste. You can always change annuals and perennials if you don't like the way they look.

Foundation trees. As for the large trees around the house, think very carefully about them before you plant. The big shapes appear at the corners of the house, usually, unless you have a particular form you want to feature elsewhere. The slope

Climbing ivy grows well on masonry surfaces, and will also grow on wooden siding as well. Structures of brick and rock, however, are particularly hospitable to ivy.

Ivy usually grows as ground cover or as a climbing vine. However, it can serve as an excellent hanging basket specimen.

Orange quince is a lone specimen in the middle of this lawn. A border of white begonias separates the tree from the surrounding grass. Quince belongs to the Cydonia genus, and should not be confused with flowering quince, of the Chaenomeles genus.

California Redwood Association

Patio setting combines ground covers, foundation plants, edgings, specimens, and vines. Ivy grows under the redwood stairway, with broad-leaved evergreen plants supplying foundation shapes near the wall at right. The needle-leaved bonsai plant in a pot adds an accent to the deck.

Photos show three different designs of espaliered trees. Against the wall of a patio, or the wall of a house, the espaliered tree can provide clean, classic lines of an arresting nature. Fruit trees are favorites for pruning and forcing into interesting shapes, and they continue to produce on a pipe or wood trellis on which they are supported.

California Redwood Association

Evergreens are mixed here against the house, one large tree that is roof height, the other a smaller plant of foundation height.

and the roll of the ground itself may give you some good ideas about the placement of big trees either near the house or away from it.

Use ornamental trees for these big shapes: dogwood, redbud, red-cedar, magnolia, and others. Be sure none of these will interfere with the windows. You can use certain tall plants to frame the doorway, but do not let them get too big or they will throw the whole front out of balance.

Be sure when planting beside the house to watch out for snow slides from the roof and icicles from the eaves. They can kill plants underneath them. Try to set them out just in front of the point directly below the edge of the eave. Some plants can recover; others cannot. It is best not to take a chance.

CARE OF FOUNDATION PLANTS. Pay strict attention to pruning all foundation plants, to make sure they stay in the proper scale and do not take over the exterior. Should a plant ever get out of hand, you should actually remove it and plant it elsewhere. It is hardly worth the fight trying to subdue it.

11 | Paths, Walls, and Terraces

A GREAT DEAL OF LANDSCAPING involves uprooting old plants and replacing them with new plants, or in sowing grass seed to produce a rolling turf, or in simply putting in trees and shrubs where there are none.

But there is another important aspect to landscaping—called "earth-moving" by engineers—that can be termed "land-shaping" by the suburban gardener.

Moving earth is part of the preparation involved in installing a house's foundation, in filling in low spots around the house when completed, and in digging for sewer and water lines. Most of this work is done before you take possession of your new house.

Even after the house is built, there is quite often need for more land-shaping—in the leveling off of the lawn area; in the design and construction of a terrace; in the building of a retaining wall to hold back eroding earth; in the digging of a place for a reflecting pool; in the construction of pathways and steps through the garden; in the terracing of several ground levels to achieve a graceful and eye-catching garden scene.

In simple situations, you can transfer dirt from one place to another with a shovel and wheelbarrow or garden cart. In more complicated situations, like leveling rugged ground for lawn planting, you may face a bit more difficult problem; usually you can handle it by using a shovel and wheelbarrow.

However, if you want to alter the contour of your lot to put in a terrace where there isn't one now, or if you want to create pathways and steps from one level to another, or if you want to smooth out a ragged terrain for a lawn, you may need to go into earth-moving by power machinery. Most homeowners prefer to hire a professional for this work, and it is therefore beyond the scope of this book.

Once the land has been graded and shaped for a particular project, you begin working with whatever materials you have planned on using. Chances are, you will be working with rock for many of these projects.

WORKING WITH ROCK. Rock, like earth, is not easy to mold to your wishes. But it serves best in its natural state, not fitted together by mortar or cement. Because rock has always coexisted with plants in their natural habitat, it is completely compatible with any landscaping scheme.

Learn to use it in your garden and you will be surprised and pleased at the effective uses to which it can be put.

In rock quarries, giant cutting tools as well as blasting powder are used to break up the virgin rock to ready it for removal. The suburban gardener can generally accomplish only the most simple processes: to break a piece into two or three separate pieces; or to nick off the edges to shape it to a desired form. When working with rock, protective goggles should always be worn. Gloves are also advisable.

Rock that can be used in the garden include:

Flagstone   Crushed rock
Slate   Gravel
Cut-stone blocks

Flagstone steps and natural rock create a perfect setting for pachysandra ground cover, azaleas, leucothoë, and a dogwood tree against the house.

Flagstone is the most popular rock; it is adaptable and versatile. If you purchase flagstone, get only the highest grade. Poor-quality stone will chip, or break.

Slate is harder than sandstone (flagstone), but it too breaks apart in flat chips. Because it is harder, it is more difficult to work, and will tend to split the way it wants to when you work it—and not necessarily the way you want it to. Use slate 1-inch thick in walks and steps. But remember it is very slippery when wet.

Cut-stone blocks are usually heavy pieces of granite, limestone, sandstone, marble, and sometimes even slate, cut roughly in huge squares. Buy blocks at least 2 inches thick in sizes at least 6 or 9 inches square. Lay these blocks like regular paving stone.

Crushed rock can be any kind of stone—granite, limestone, slate, or marble—and it comes in different colors along with solid white. Bluestone—actually a type of sandstone—is gray-blue in color. Marble chips are pieces of marble crushed to uniform size. Pink stone is composed of crushed pieces of pink granite. Pieces of concrete sidewalk can be broken up into attractive crushed rock, too.

Gravel can be any kind of granules of rock broken down to very small sizes (but not as small as sand). It tends to be unattractive and is the least preferable rock for use on walks, terraces, driveways, and any kind of yard surface. Don't use it for play areas.

FLAGSTONE. Flagstone is a type of sandstone or hard shale that splits into thin flakes when quarried. The word "flag" refers to the shape of the stone and not the type of rock.

Most flags used in the suburban garden can be purchased in varying thicknesses; a thickness about 1½ inches is usually best for walks and terraces.

Sandstone is a soft type of rock, easier to work with than tougher ones like granite, slate, and marble. However, even sandstone can be tricky. The most malleable piece of flag is very brittle and will splinter at the wrong place exactly as glass does in the hands of an inexperienced glazier.

Cutting flagstone. To cut flagstone, use a stone-worker's chisel; it is about 2 or 3 inches wide at the cutting edge. Use a hammer to strike the chisel; use some force.

To cut, first mark a guide line along the rock where you want it to break. Place the rock on a hard, flat surface.

Then work the chisel along the line until you have scored the line visibly into the stone. Continue to move the chisel along that line again and again. As the scoring line becomes more deeply imbedded in the rock, hit the chisel harder and harder. Soon the rock will break along the scored line.

If possible, avoid doing a lot of cutting. It is quite aggravating to have rock break at the wrong point; and it is apt to unless you are skilled or lucky.

Nibbling. Hammer and chisel are necessary to cut a piece of rock in two or three pieces, as explained above. If you have a piece of sandstone that is almost the form you want, but not quite, try nibbling it into shape.

Nibbling is simply the act of pounding away at the edge of a piece of rock with the hammer's head, breaking or nibbling away at the edge until you get the outline or border you want.

LAYING A FLAGSTONE WALK. When you purchase flagstone, you usually can specify the thickness you want—and the rock itself will be at least within that general area. You cannot count on all the thicknesses being exactly uniform. Tell the dealer how many square feet of ground you want to cover, not how many pounds of rock you want.

In building a flagstone walk, you will waste a great deal of stone if you demand a formal appearance, with straight-edged pieces and uniform small joints between. An informal walkway with random pieces will cost a lot less and will take less cutting time and waste less stone.

Laying out the walk. First of all, plan the pathway through your garden area. Keep the walk as level as you can, letting it meander or go straight where it takes a natural bent.

A pathway 18 inches wide is actually big enough if it is intended for the use of one person at a time. If you want a pathway that will permit two people to stroll side by side, you must make it 4½ feet to 5 feet wide.

When you have the pathway well in mind, lay it out by pounding stakes into the ground along the proposed borders.

Flagstone walk of random-shaped pieces has a simplicity and naturalness that blends with the lawn, driveway, and foliage.

Flagstone deck can be made of odd-shaped pieces or, as here, of cut rectangular slabs.

Laying the bed. Next comes the job of laying the bed for the rock. Dig up all the dirt inside the border stakes to a depth of an inch or so. Make the bottom of the bed as level as possible, and tamp it down, after removing uneven stones, weeds, and roots.

Place a layer of sand, cinders, and/or gravel on the surface of the excavation, and level the surface of the fill as flat as possible. Tamp it down.

Laying the flagstone. Select pieces of flagstone that will fit within the border lines of the walkway as close as possible to one another with fairly uniform spaces between.

To make an accurate fit with an even space between two borders, lay stone *A* over stone *B* where they will meet. Mark the border of *A* on *B*. Cut along the line on *B*, or nibble the edge away until it corresponds to the border of *A*.

Then lay the two stones in the base with the desired width between.

Proceed with all the stones along the pathway, laying each where it will ultimately rest.

Juggle each stone about until it fits tightly to the base fill. Step on it to be sure that it does not rock. If a stone rocks, lift it out and readjust the fill below until the flag fits snugly into the base material.

When all the flags are firm, add soil where the joints appear between. Tamp the soil in tightly and make sure the stones do not rock.

Finishing the pathway. Plant grass in the soil between the flagstones. If you want a more informal effect, plant low-growing, mat-forming plants—thyme, sedum, ajuga, veronica repens, and so on. Water the seeds and protect them with mulch. Remove the stakes at the side of the pathway and wait for the grass or ground cover to grow.

A similar pathway can be made using slate, or any other kind of rock you wish.

LAYING A STEPPING-STONE WALK. While a flagstone or slate walk is generally designed as a continuous-width walkway, you can put in a more informal type by placing stones of any thickness and shape every 18 inches without a thought of making them fit into each other's borders.

This jaunty walkway is called a stepping-stone walk. It can be straight, curved, or meandering. You don't even need to use flag or slate. Any stone that has one flat side and is at least 1 to 1½ feet in diameter will do.

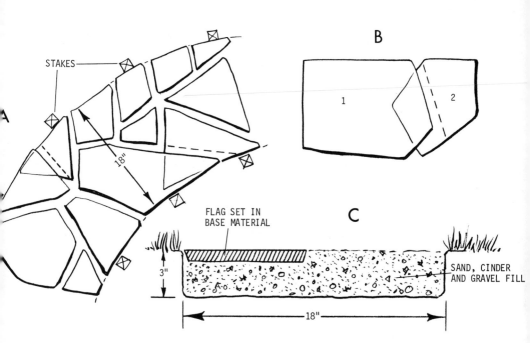

Diagram A shows how to lay out a flagstone path. Borders are marked by stakes about 12 inches apart along 18-inch-wide pathway. To mark stone for cutting (B), lay stone #1 over stone #2. Mark the cut on stone #2 along the edge of stone #1, making sure there will be sufficient border space between pieces when laid. Cross section C shows how to make a bed for a walk by digging a cut 3 inches deep and 18 inches wide, and filling it with sand, cinders, and gravel so flagstone has a level place to rest.

Laying out the path. First lay out the pathway, using the procedure outlined above.

Select random stepping stones and lay them exactly as you want them on top of the grass or ground.

Once the rocks are laid out, make sure the centers are about 18 inches apart—the average slow-walking pace of the average person—and then check again to be sure each stone is exactly where you want it.

Preparing the bed. Mark the turf around the edges of each stone by pounding in tiny splinter stakes. Remove the stones. Dig out the area inside the marked borders and try to shape each to take the bottom of the stone that will sit there. Make the hole about one inch deeper than it should be to hold the stone with the top flush with the turf.

Laying random stones. Now pour an inch of sand in the bottom of each hole, shaping it to the bottom of the stone.

Lay the first stepping stone in and set it in position so that it does not rock even when you try to move it. If it rocks, take it up and rearrange the sand and soil beneath. When the stone sits in snugly and will not rock, press the soil in around the sides and edges with a firm hand. Replace any grass that might have been torn up.

163

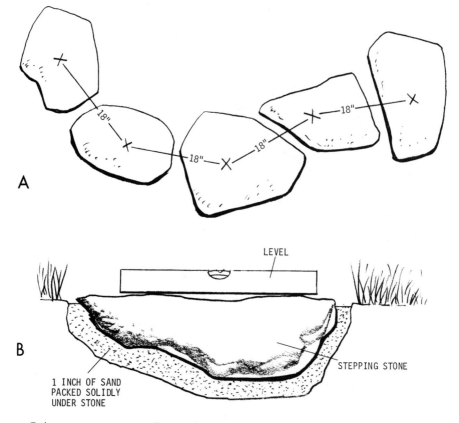

To lay out stepping-stone walk correctly, make sure that center or near-center of each stone is exactly 18 inches from its neighbor. Then place stones as shown in A. Dig into sod, B, fill the excavation with one inch of sand, and lay the stone in. Use a level to position the stone.

LAYING A PEBBLE WALK. Creek-washed pebbles or crushed rock of any kind make an excellent walkway surface. They can be used to a depth of 3 or 4 inches.

Rock of all types is available commercially for use in a walkway: bluestone, whitestone, crushed marble, marble chips, granite chips, and so on.

The main problem with laying crushed rock or pebbles is one of drainage. Rain water or overflow it liable to settle in the rocks and remain in the middle of the pathway with no way out. For that reason, a porous base is needed to afford good outflow.

Laying out the path. Lay out the path in the manner previously described. Once the marking stakes are in place, dig up the turf or ground in between the stakes to a depth of 7 inches.

Level out the bottom of the excavation, removing all odd-shaped rocks and roots, making it as flat as possible. Tamp it down.

Filling in the base. Fill the hole up with about 6 inches of throw-away crushed rock, or cinders, with gravel added at the top if you have it available.

Round the top of the base so that the center is about an inch higher than the

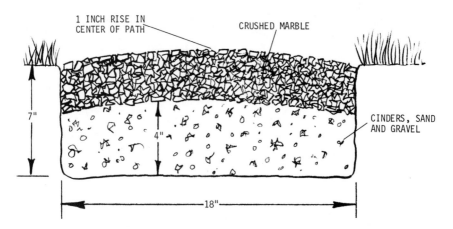

Elevation shows pathway made of crushed marble, crushed rock, or river pebbles. The excavation should be 7 inches deep, 18 inches wide. Form the base of the cinders, sand, and gravel with a 1-inch rise in the middle. When packing in pathway material, carry out the 1-inch rise, called camber, which will aid in drainage.

borders. This will afford natural drainage when the water seeps in through the rocks above the gravel.

Laying the crushed rock. Now place the crushed rock, crushed marble, or creek-washed pebbles on top of the cinder-gravel base.

Lay each rock in carefully, placing it individually. If you simply dump the rocks onto the base, they will not fit properly and will settle later, leaving gaps and sometimes depressions in the pathway.

Place the biggest sizes solidly on the cinder base. Then fill in the gaps between them with smaller pebbles, building up the rock surface in this manner to a thickness of about 3 inches.

Let the surface of the path extend a bit above the surface of the turf.

Keep the center of the path about an inch above the borders to aid in efficient drainage.

TANBARK PATHWAY. Tanbark is especially suitable for a woodsy pathway. This material looks like shredded wood pulp and fits very well under trees on a walkway. It resembles a natural forest carpet.

Actually, tanbark is the bark of the chestnut oak or the hemlock. It has a brown, red-yellow hue, and is excellent as a mulch, a ground cover, and a footing for a pathway.

To build a good tanbark pathway, you must be sure to provide good drainage.

Mark off the pathway by driving stakes in the ground along the borders. Dig out the dirt in between to a depth of 3 inches, and clear the bottom out, removing weeds, roots, and rocks. Tamp down the dirt.

Lay in tanbark to a depth of 3 inches. Soak the tanbark with a hose. Roll the wet tanbark with a good lawn roller, making it sink down well into its bed.

LAYING A CRUSHED MARBLE EDGING. Crushed marble can be used to excellent effect in an edging along an asphalt driveway, a dirt pathway, or even a gravel area.

Crushed marble surfacing is used here as a border along the tennis court. At left, blue fescue joins with begonias to give color and shape as edging plants along steps of crushed rock and railroad ties.

You can procure bags of crushed marble from any garden supply store. All you need to hold the chips in place are two-by-four borders, preferably of redwood.

Start out by marking the shape of the edging area with stakes pushed into the ground. Dig out all the grass sod and dirt to a depth of about 3 inches. The idea is to keep the level of the edging material below the surface of the contiguous grass, enabling you to mow up to the path without any hindrance.

Lay in the two-by-fours and remove any extra dirt until there is a slight gap between the redwood timber and the sod next to it. Then nail the two-by-fours together, filling in any gaps with dirt.

Rake the bed carefully until it is level, and then tamp it down. Get rid of weeds and debris.

Lay the crushed marble chips in one by one, starting with the biggest ones first. Then put in the smaller ones to fill the spaces between. The level of the crushed marble should be just about the same as the level of the lawn alongside it.

RETAINING WALL. Where there are sharp differences in elevation in a lot, a retaining wall may be essential to keep soil from eroding in flood weather. The best kind of retaining wall is one built of natural rock, without mortar between. Called a "dry wall," a natural retaining wall should never be higher than 5 feet in a geographical area where frost action occurs in the earth. Such a retaining wall must be considerably thicker at the base than at the top.

The wall base. Start by marking off the area where you want the wall. The width of the base of the wall should be about one-third of the ultimate height of the wall.

Now dig a trench about 18 inches deep where the bottom of the wall will rest. Fill this trench with gravel and/or crushed rock. Gravel makes a suitable footing for a wall. If you are building the wall in very clayey soil, you may not need a footing at all, since there will be little settling after the wall is built.

Used in off-beat fashion, crushed marble acts as an accent to strict formalism of garden surrounded by round brick border. Broad-leaved evergreens form simulated ground cover around the formal circle.

Retaining wall made of cut rock creates a dramatic dividing line across this property. The square lines of the rock stand out against the natural surroundings.

Rock can be stacked in the form of a wall and featured just for the sake of its rugged beauty.

Rock for the wall. Select rocks that are flat and narrow or square in shape. They must be chosen to fit closely together. Rounded stones do not make good dry-wall material. It is best to use large rocks with abrupt angles and relatively flat surfaces. They are stronger and less apt to slide.

If you have rounded stones that you would like to use, chip off the curves with a stone chisel, or break round rocks in two for easier shaping. Use stone native to your region.

Building the wall. Start with the lowest row of the wall, using the largest rocks you have on hand. Pitch the rocks at a slight angle, slanting from the outside of the wall to the inside and down. If the stones do not slant this way, water from above will flow down through the middle and out between the stones, taking soil along with it.

Between the two outside rows of stones, fill in dirt. Then add a few inches of soil to the top of the first run. Place about 6 inches of dirt in back of each rock or stone and pack it in firmly to avoid air pockets and loose soil that will cause frost heaves.

The second row of rocks needs careful positioning. Place each rock not on top of one in the lower row, but in between two, so that its weight is borne by two rocks and not one rock and the soil.

Continue in this way to the top, placing each rock in a horizontal position. When the wall is completed, its weight will be carried by the rocks, and there will be horizontal crevices in the wall. In these crevices you can grow plants. In fact, it is best to plant something here to keep the soil from chance erosion.

OTHER USES OF NATURAL ROCK. Like a tree or shrub, rock can be used in a suburban landscape as a single specimen. Selection and placement of a good rock is a highly creative art. It calls for judgment and an appreciation of the way nature places rocks in mountainous terrain.

Be selective in picking out the rock you want to feature. If the rock is large enough you can use it as the pivot for a driveway turnaround, or even as a buffer in the middle of the yard to divide a flower garden from a vegetable garden.

Two "steps" of rock, arranged to simulate an old-fashioned stile in the woods, create an interesting garden accent.

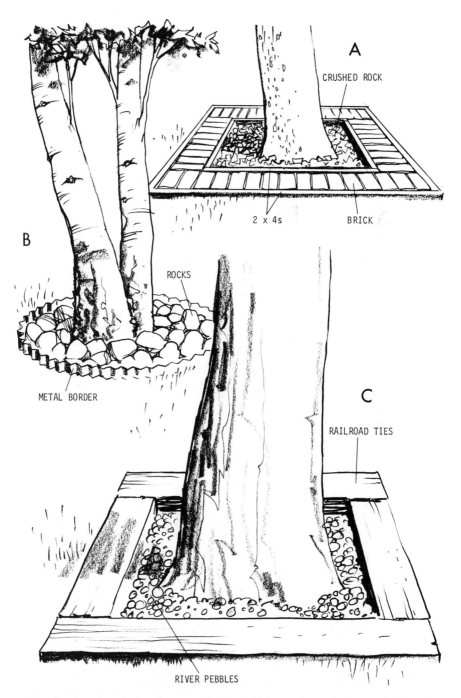

Tree borders of crushed rocks or smooth river pebbles can be made in several different ways. *A* shows a square border of crushed rock enclosed in border of sunken 2-by-4s. *B* shows a border of stones enclosed by a metal hoop-like circle. *C* shows washed river pebbles enclosed by a square of old railroad ties.

A large rock boulder can be used as the basis for repetitive patterns in retaining walls, walks, and in the wall of the house itself. Such an accent will be quite pleasing in its rhythmic reappearance in various other patterns, sizes, and textures.

Like anything else, a rock specimen can be used as a focal point for a whole yard, or merely as a screen, liner, or border for something bigger.

Tree borders. A tree must be protected from physical injury at the base of the trunk or it will ail and die. Crushed rock placed around the tree is one of the best kinds of protection.

You can border the crushed rock area with a square formed by buried 2-by-4 timbers. If that square is not large enough, lay bricks outside the square, forming a larger area, bordered again by 2-by-4s buried in the ground.

Instead of crushed rock, you can use large river-washed stones. Make a border of timbers, or even use a metal border if you like, to keep the rock and lawn separate. Plant the stones low enough so they will not interfere with a mower.

Dig a fairly deep hole around a tree, fill it with crushed stone, and then make a box of railroad ties to add a dramatic accent to any large tree. The rocks will keep out the weeds, and prevent the dirt from eroding toward the trunk.

Rock, in conjunction with wood, with brick, or with cement blocks, can be used in many ways to protect tree trunks at ground level—from injury by lawnmowers and from overgrowth by weeds and competing plants.

Driveways. A driveway made of crushed rock is a thing of the past because a rock drive usually caves in during rainy weather and the rock simply sinks into the earth and vanishes.

However, crushed rock is an excellent driveway *surface*. Some builders now construct a regular asphalt driveway and lay a 1-inch thickness of crushed rock over the asphalt when it is hot. This surface gives the driveway an excellent texture, preventing skidding and sliding in icy weather.

The same can be true of an asphalt walkway, if you are afraid crushed rock by itself will wash away or sink into the ground. (It won't if you put a base of sand and cinders underneath.)

Ground cover. One of the most dramatic new uses of crushed rock is as a ground cover, rather than grass or low-growth plants. Crushed rock applied in sufficient depth, usually over a bed of sand, will retard weed growth completely. The crushed rock can be compacted under pressure to prevent any shifting and to support mowing equipment.

You can use a crushed rock cover for a terrace, too, as explained later in this chapter.

Mulch. Crushed rock can also be used for mulch. As such it keeps out weeds and retains moisture and heat in the ground that would otherwise escape. Rock makes a very good-looking mulch, and can be used with any kinds of flowers, shrubs, and trees.

First lay sheets of plastic over the entire area of ground where you intend to put in the rock mulch.

Cover that with a mixture of crushed rock and sand to fill in the spaces between the rock. The mulch should be about 4 to 6 inches thick.

The plastic underlayment will smother any weed growth from beneath, and the weeds that spring up in the crushed rock and sand itself can be easily removed.

To prevent rock mulch from drifting, use heavy metal edging material around its perimeter. Bend the edging material to whatever shape you want, and sink it into the

Smooth river pebbles have been used here as a substitute for lawn or ground cover next to the house. Plants and needle-leaved evergreen carry out the theme.

ground, allowing it to extend no more than 1 inch above the earth. This edging will keep the crushed rock from spreading out onto the grass.

Rock gardens. A high and dry site that has no shade and receives an abundance of sunshine is an ideal spot for a rock garden. Casual and informal, a rock garden, like a flower bed of annuals or perennials, is an adjunct to basic landscaping and outside the scope of this book.

TERRACES AND PATIOS. The increase in the amount of time spent in outdoor living has heightened the prestige of the suburban terrace and patio. In fact, this area of the homesite has become probably the most important part of the average garden.

The terrace or patio is actually an open-air living room, larger than its interior counterpart and furnished with plants and grass.

In landscaping terms, the function of the terrace is to unite the house with the surrounding trees, shrubs, and ground cover; essentially, to forge a link between the natural outdoor life and the artificial indoor life.

It takes great skill to design and plant a terrace properly.

Terrace vs. patio. Although the terms terrace and patio are used interchangeably by many homeowners, a technical difference between the two does exist. Actually, in some instances, the word deck is used in place of either terrace or patio.

Patio is the oldest term and comes from the Spanish word for "court," or "open space"—that is, the open part of the villa or house exposed to the elements. Spain borrowed the idea of the central outdoor garden from the Moors, who built their houses in a U-shape around the garden, with a wall across the back.

California was first settled by Spanish missionaries who brought the patio from their homeland. Later, the patio became an open garden attached to the rear of a ranch-type house, and fenced in on 3 sides.

Terrace, from "*terra,*" (land) simply means a flat piece of land that is used for recreation or pleasure. An older use of the word implied a series of different levels of flat land, one above the next, used by farmers in planting crops on slopes. Now the word means a flat piece of land, usually paved or planted with grass, attached to a habitation, and used for outdoor recreation.

A typical pattern for a flagstone terrace or deck. This should be drawn before laying the flags. Number each piece on the bottom as soon as you place it in the plan. For stones that are the wrong shape or size, draw a dotted line in chalk across them, indicating cuts.

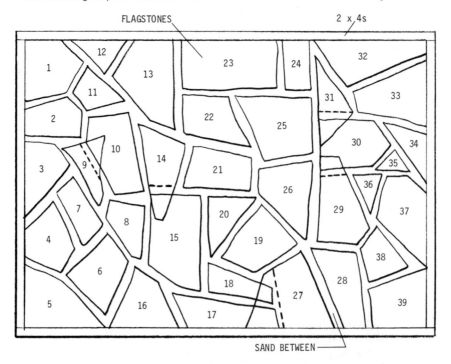

Deck is a platform made of wooden planks fastened together, extending out from a house into a yard. It can be at ground-floor level, or even as high as the top of the house.

Presently, each of these three terms is applied to a recreational area either attached to or near the back of a house, extending out into the yard and acting as an important part of the garden scene.

Placing a terrace. Since a terrace surface must be level, you should plan to place the terrace where it will take the least earth-moving to make it ready for paving. If your yard is undulating and uneven, plan to elevate a portion of the terrain for the terrace. Set it off from the rest of the yard by slopes planted with ground cover or low-growth plants. If it is necessary to move earth in order to obtain a level area, follow the instructions at the beginning of this chapter.

Terrace paving materials. Land-shaping is involved in constructing a terrace, particularly in paving it. Besides grass turf, the following materials are only some of those used:

Flagstone	Gravel
Slate	Wood blocks
Stone	Blacktop
Masonry	Tanbark
Marble chips	Pine needles

PAVING A TERRACE WITH NATURAL ROCK. It is not within the province of this book to explain how to pour a concrete floor or an asphalt blacktop surface for a terrace or how to build a deck. However, it is appropriate to explain how to pave a terrace with natural rock: flagstone; slate; crushed rock; stone.

Any kind of natural rock surface used for a terrace should be set in a bed of sand — unless there is no possibility of freezing weather.

How to lay out a terrace. When the ground has been leveled satisfactorily, lay out the border of the terrace by marking it with stakes pounded into the ground. Plan the terrace so that it will slope slightly to take care of drainage. Even with sand as an absorbent bed, a great deal of water will accumulate if there is not a normal flow to take it away from the slab. A slope of 1 inch in 4 to 8 feet should be enough.

At the borders of the terrace area, dig 2-inch slots in the ground 4 inches deep, and lay in 2-by-4 timbers to outline the terrace's shape. Lay them so that the top of the 2-by-4s will be flush at the top with the flagstones when laid.

Beginning with one 2-by-4 border, lay flagstones exactly as you want them to appear when the terrace is finished. Arrange the flags so that about an inch of space lies between them. For a neater look, choose straight edges to make the border.

Excavate the terrace area to be filled by flagstones to a depth of 6 inches, planning a 1-inch drop in 4 to 8 feet for drainage. Slope terrace either from the center to the edges or from one end to another, as convenient. Border with 2-by-4 lumber.

If some stones need cutting to fit, lay them in so that they overlap. Mark a cutting line exactly where you want it to be.

Now tip up each flagstone and number it on the bottom, beginning with 1 on the top end of the first border. Continue numbering up and down each row until you have finished.

Now take up the stones and pile them in order outside the area of the terrace.

Laying the base. Dig all the dirt out of the terrace area inside the border timbers to a depth of at least 6 inches. Smooth the ground as level as possible, removing all odd-shaped rocks and roots.

Mix cinder, gravel, and crushed stone together, and pour it over the bottom of the entire area to a depth of at least 4 inches.

Smooth over the base by dragging a board across it. Tamp the material down carefully to get it level. Pour 2 inches of sand on top of that base. Smooth the sand. Tamp it down. Soak it with a fine spray of water. When the sand dries, fill in all the spots that have sunken down in the soaking.

Check the entire area with a carpenter's level on a 2-by-4 timber to make sure the sand base is level.

Laying the paving. Start laying the flagstone pieces in the order of their numbers along the first border. Lay in all the pieces against the 2-by-4 timber before going on to the next row.

Lay in the first piece and make sure that it does not rock or move when you step on it. If tamping it into the sand with a block of wood between hammer head and flag-

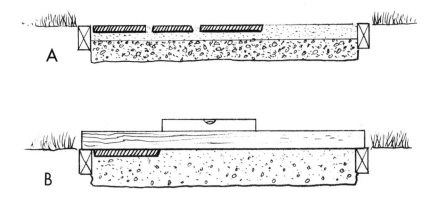

After area is excavated, fill the base first with a 4-inch mix of sand, cinders, and gravel. Then lay on 2 inches of fine sand, which will act as filling base for the flags. *B* shows how to check the level of each stone as it is set in the sand. *C* shows how to tamp the stone in place, using block of wood to protect the surface of the stone.

stone does not secure it, remove the flagstone and shift the sand underneath until it will hold the piece firmly.

When it is firm, lay a straightedge 2-by-4 timber from one border to the other, across the top of the flagstone, and lay the carpenter's level on top of that. Check the flagstone for its position.

When the flagstone is both level and firm, move on to the next and repeat the process.

When you come to a piece that needs to be cut, proceed as explained earlier in this chapter.

As you set in each new flagstone and determine that it is level with the borders, use the carpenter's level and check it with each of its neighbors.

Finishing the slab. When all the pieces of flagstone are laid, dump random piles of sand across the slab and sweep it into the cracks between the flags. Brush off any excess and water down the entire slab.

If you want to, you can leave in the 2-by-4s as a border for the terrace; or lift them out when the flags are laid and replace the soil and grass that was removed.

Note: If you plan to lay slate, stones, crushed rock, or any kind of rock pavement, treat it exactly as you would flagstone.

Remember that slate has brighter colors, but that it is fragile and that it is very slippery when wet. Avoid using it on a terrace that is subject to traffic and stormy weather.

Material like tanbark or pine needles can be placed directly on the ground for a terrace surface; it need not be as carefully adjusted as flagstone or slate pieces.

If you are planting a grass surface for a terrace, level the terrace first as explained and proceed with the grass planting as discussed in Chapter 2.

In areas not subject to winter freezing, you can lay flagstones directly in the ground. Simply cut out sod to fit the flag and lay in each piece as described in this chapter. Use a carpenter's level and a 2-by-4 to keep the slab level.

PLANTING A TERRACE. Whatever the surface of the terrace is paved with—concrete, natural rock, redwood, or turf—it must blend in with the plantings surrounding it.

Planting a terrace demands skill and imagination. You must remember that the area should be a medium for harmonizing the outdoors with the indoors.

If there is an excess of sun on the terrace, you can plant one or more trees in strategic spots: crabapple or flowering dogwood for shade, or even a larger tree like a maple.

You may not need shade of any kind, but rather shelter from the elements. In that case, an evergreen hedge or a line of windbreak trees can be put along the windward side of the terrace.

If you do not need shelter from the elements, you should place plants to define the area of the terrace to the greatest advantage. Holly trees and yew will mark the borders or a paving clearly, or you may line the edge of it with specimens growing in planters.

If your terrace is made of stepping stones you can plant the crevices either with grass, or with a ground cover like thyme, sandwort, bugleweed, rock-cress, or creeping speedwell.

If you have a stone retaining wall defining one border of the terrace, plant it with a wall garden.

California Redwood Association

Huge round stepping stones made of redwood tree sections have been used effectively in a mulch-like base of broken rock. Fence, deck, and uprights are redwood also.

Prescolite Mfg. Corp.

Long-needled pine tree combines with broad-leaved evergreens to act as a foundation planting near a wood fence. Chipped wood mulch has been substituted for lawn over a large area of the patio.

TERRACE PLANTS

SHADE TREES

COMMON NAME	BOTANICAL NAME	HEIGHT	ZONE
Carolina Silverbell	*Halesia carolina*	30'	5
Chinese Fringetree	*Chionanthus retusus*	18'	5
Flowering Dogwood	*Cornus florida*	40'	4
Magnolia	*Magnolia grandiflora*	40'	7
Pin Oak	*Quercus palustris*	75'	4
Red Maple	*Acer rubrum*	120'	3
Serviceberry (Shadbush)	*Amelanchier canadensis*	60'	4
Siberian Crabapple	*Malus baccata*	50'	2

EVERGREENS

COMMON NAME	BOTANICAL NAME	HEIGHT	ZONE
Canadian Yew	*Taxus canadensis*	60'	6
Dwarf White Pine	*Pinus strobus Brevifolia*	7'	3
Holly	*Ilex opaca*	45'	5
Scarlet Firethorn	*Pyracantha coccinea*	6'	6

SHRUBS

COMMON NAME	BOTANICAL NAME	HEIGHT	ZONE
Dwarf Rhododendron	*Rhododendron* species		
Glossy Abelia	*Abelia grandiflora*	5'	5
Hybrid Bluebeard	*Caryopteris clandonensis*	4'	6
Lilac	*Syringa* species		
Viburnum	*Viburnum* species		

PLANTS

COMMON NAME	BOTANICAL NAME	HEIGHT	ZONE
Begonia	*Begonia* species		
Common Heliotrope	*Heliotropium arborescens*	4–6'	10
Common Fuchsia	*Fuchsia hybrida*	3–5'	10
Geranium	*Geranium* species		
Impatiens	*Impatiens* species		

GROUND COVERS

COMMON NAME	BOTANICAL NAME	HEIGHT	ZONE
Bugleweed	*Ajuga reptans*	4–12"	2–3
Canby Pachistima	*Paxistima canbyi*	12"	5
Creeping Speedwell	*Veronica repens*	4"	5
Mother-of-Thyme	*Thymus serpyllum*	ground	3
Rock-cress	*Arabis* species		
Sandwort	*Arenaria* species	ground	3
Trailing Lantana	*Lantana montevidensis*	2'	10

GARDEN STEPS. In a homesite that has several different ground elevations, it is important to provide easy access to the various levels by means of sturdy and well-built steps. This is one of the most important of all landshaping operations; unless you can move unimpeded about your yard, you have lost use of most of it.

You can always have steps built by a contractor, cast in concrete for permanence. But it is always nicer to build your own steps with natural materials designed to fit in with the original garden plants.

Steps are made of smooth flag-stone treads set onto cut-rock risers. Borders feature chipped wood mulch and cotoneaster evergreen accent plantings, scattered with marigolds to lend color.

Outdoor steps rise much more gradually than indoor steps. In designing garden steps, plan to use a broad tread and a very low riser. A garden step tread is quite often wider than 12 inches.

Steps should be designed to fit the terrain. They can go in a straight line or in a curving line. You can even design a switchback if you have a quick rise to span.

Be sure not to plan long, uninterrupted flights of steps. Such a lengthy rise is tiring, and aesthetically monotonous. Remember that outdoor steps should look at least as interesting as the garden around them.

A stroll up outdoor steps should prove to be diverse, with continued eye-catching views as you walk along.

Break up long flights with platforms made of varying materials, not only to slow the upward climb and afford rest for the stroller, but also to give the eye more interesting materials to look at.

There are many different kinds of materials available for use in building steps:

Concrete	Crushed rock
Brick	Rustic logs
Paving blocks	Railroad ties
Flagstone	Grass sod
Slate	

These materials are only a few of the many possibilities open to you. Try to select something that harmonizes with the terrace, retaining wall, rocks, plants, driveway, walk, or fence that borders the steps or is visible from them. If possible, repeat some material used in these other areas.

For example, if you have redwood planters visible on a terrace slab, line the steps with redwood planks; if you have begonias visible in a garden bed nearby, border the steps with more begonias.

The width of the path to the steps should determine the width of the steps. If you have no pathway to guide you, design the steps to the same width advisable for a pathway: 18 inches wide for one person; 4½ to 5 feet wide for more than one person.

If there are a lot of curves in the steps, you can even add an extra 6 to 12 inches

Crushed rock steps with railroad tie risers are bordered by low-lying evergreen shrubs, juniper and cotoneaster, and tiny begonias. Pampas grass specimen at left foreground adds a spiky naturalness.

without wrecking the design. Be sure that the treads are wide enough to accommodate a full footfall and more. The tread at the *inside* of a curve should be at least 10 to 12 inches long. You don't want any broken legs or sprained ankles from falls in the garden because a tread isn't wide enough.

Because of the infinite variation in types of terrain and in slopes and rises in land, there are no hard and fast rules for laying out steps.

However, it is necessary to build secure steps in order to avoid accidents on them.

Flagstone steps. Large flagstones—2 feet wide by 2 feet in length—are excellent materials for steps. Set these in the ground and make them completely secure by tamping them into place firmly.

Place a 2 by 6 plank under the end of the step as a riser, if the step is not solid enough.

Crushed rock. To hold in the rock, place a riser, either a 2-by-6 timber or a railroad tie, at the end of the tread.

Secure the plank or tie, either by digging it in solidly, or by pounding in stakes to hold it in place.

Dig out the dirt behind the riser to a depth of 4 inches and put in the crushed rock, placing it carefully in for the tread. Level the crushed rock and tamp it in place.

If the rock pieces begin to shift, you can procure a type of clear adhesive at a garden supply store that can be poured over the rocks to keep them firmly in place. The adhesive is strong but does not obscure the color or texture of the crushed rock.

If the steps are subject to freezing and thawing, or if the steps are subject to a lot of usage, it is best to secure them with adhesive.

Crushed rock, river pebbles, and gravel can be made into steps in the above manner.

Railroad ties. You can build steps using railroad ties as risers. Simply lay the ties in the ground, and secure them. Be sure to plant them firmly. Pound stakes deep into the earth at the ends of the ties, and nail the ties to the stakes if they are apt to move. This will prevent the ties from slipping and turning.

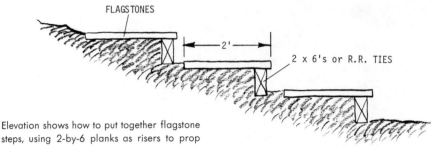

Elevation shows how to put together flagstone steps, using 2-by-6 planks as risers to prop them up.

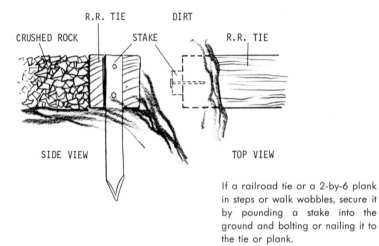

If a railroad tie or a 2-by-6 plank in steps or walk wobbles, secure it by pounding a stake into the ground and bolting or nailing it to the tie or plank.

Loose railroad tie in steps can be secured by bolting 2-by-6 braces to it and extending them back into the earth out of sight. Both railroad tie and braces will hold in the crushed rock or other material in step.

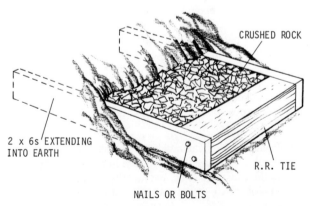

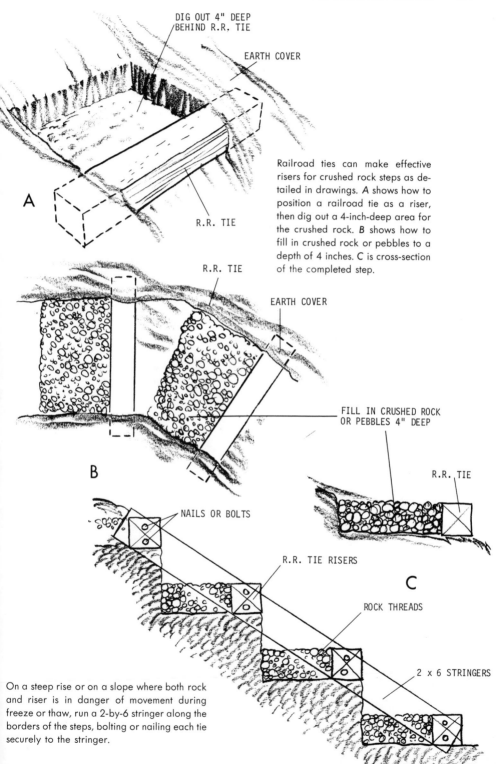

DIG OUT 4" DEEP
BEHIND R.R. TIE

EARTH COVER

A

R.R. TIE

Railroad ties can make effective
risers for crushed rock steps as detailed in drawings. A shows how to
position a railroad tie as a riser,
then dig out a 4-inch-deep area for
the crushed rock. B shows how to
fill in crushed rock or pebbles to a
depth of 4 inches. C is cross-section
of the completed step.

R.R. TIE

EARTH COVER

FILL IN CRUSHED ROCK
OR PEBBLES 4" DEEP

B

R.R. TIE

NAILS OR BOLTS

R.R. TIE RISERS

C

ROCK THREADS

2 x 6 STRINGERS

On a steep rise or on a slope where both rock
and riser is in danger of movement during
freeze or thaw, run a 2-by-6 stringer along the
borders of the steps, bolting or nailing each tie
securely to the stringer.

You can get a very rustic effect by using good-looking and interesting wood logs for steps, exactly like railroad ties. Secure the logs in the earth with stakes the same way.

If the grade is steep, you would be wise to attach both logs and ties to running planks along the sides, just as treads and risers are secured to the stringers in regular wooden stairs construction.

Grass steps. If you have good solid turf and wish to maintain a completely rustic effect, you can use grass sod for steps.

Use small risers of wood, railroad ties, logs, concrete, bricks, or any kind of rock to define the end of the tread. This border will keep the grass and soil from eroding.

Do not try to plant grass on bare earth to make steps. Buy sod and roll it in, using the protection of wood or rock risers to keep the sod in place.

A pathway or walk made out of grass needs constant maintenance. But if you can keep it up, nothing is better.

Do not forget that if you have a path or steps planted in turf, it needs constant sunlight.

Planting steps. With natural steps, you can use rugged rock-garden type plants at the base of the risers; thyme, sedum, and so on. Even ground covers like myrtle and English ivy can be trained to grow along the base.

Flowering varieties of foliage along the sides of the steps will add to the natural appearance.

Shrubs and flowers will soften the harsh outline of the construction and will frame it in an inviting manner.

You can even place shrubs or flowers in planters along the way if you wish. There are many different ways to make steps attractive. Use your imagination.

12 | Garden Tools

MAN HAS ALWAYS USED AGRICULTURAL tools for planting trees and growing food. At first these tools were made of animal bones, then of stone, and finally of metal. Up until recently, these tools were hand tools, applied to the work by the muscle of man. Now technology has added another concept to tools – power.

Garden tools have not yet made a total transition to power. In fact, every single gardening activity can still be performed by hand. Yet power tools are of tremendous aid to the suburban gardener who does not have all the time in the world to putter about.

Some planting and maintenance operations you may prefer to do by hand, others by power. The following rundown on garden tools includes most of those you might want to use in a typical suburban situation.

In this chapter gardening operations have been divided arbitrarily into these following nine actions:

(1) Digging	(4) Spreading	(7) Raking
(2) Loading	(5) Cutting	(8) Prying
(3) Transporting	(6) Chopping	(9) Spraying

DIGGING TOOLS. Every gardener must have a spade, a fork, and a trowel. No matter how academic it may seem, a discussion on digging tools is in order.

Both spade and fork are used for loading as well as digging, but each is primarily designed for digging. The correct tool to use for loading is a shovel or pitchfork, each of which is a modification of the digging spade and garden fork.

Spade and shovel. In common usage, the terms spade and shovel are carelessly interchanged. However, each tool has a different design and purpose.

The spade is designed to cut into the ground. It has a short handle, and a sharp blade. It usually is equipped with foot holds on top of the blade. The blade is mounted almost parallel to the handle. It is meant to turn ground, bury weeds, dig out shrubs, excavate holes for plantings, and dig up compost and manure.

The shovel is designed to load and carry. It has a long handle that can be used as a fulcrum for lifting. It has a blade that is not sharp, but that is rounded for holding material. It has no foot holds, and the blade lies at an angle from the handle. The tool is meant to load and transport loose materials from one place to another, or to place materials in a wheelbarrow or cart for further transportation.

Trouble arises when you use a shovel to dig a hole in the ground. Since the tool is not made for cutting and digging, it can give you a bad backache. You have to force the handle way out from your body to insert the blade into the ground at a vertical angle. In pulling the handle back and lifting the load of dirt, you use more back muscles than you should. In lifting dirt from the hole, you work with a handle that is too long for the job performed.

However, in certain rocky ground, it is sometimes useful to use the loading shovel as a hole-digger. You can use the fulcrum of the handle to help pry rocks loose in hardened soil.

Spade's digging blade is almost parallel with the handle to provide for greater cutting force downward into the earth. Note reinforced edges where foot pressure is applied when digging.

True Temper Corp.

Shovel is designed for carrying material and has long handle at a slight angle to curved blade. Loads of dirt, leaves, and debris can be carried easily or loaded on or off carrying carts. Note lack of reinforced edges on blade.

Likewise, it is asking for trouble to use a digging spade as a loading shovel. The long handle on the loading shovel provides an extensive reach as well as good leverage. If you use a short-handled digging spade for loading work, you will have to strain to throw the material any distance. Also, the material will continually slide off the flatter surface of the digging spade.

To make matters most confusing, there is a type of shovel called a digging shovel that is used for some kinds of digging. The digging shovel, like the spade, has a shorter handle than the loading shovel. The blade of the digging shovel is bent at less of an angle than the blade of the loading shovel.

The digging shovel is the best garden tool to use for moving shrubbery. Because the angle of the blade is shallow, you can stand closer to the shrub and dig straight down without interference of the branches. You can also use the blade for chopping roots off.

Generally speaking, the short-handled spade or digging shovel is the proper implement to use in digging in the earth; and the long-handled shovel is the proper implement to use in loading or transporting material from one place to another.

Garden fork and pitch fork. Some confusion exists between the garden fork and pitch fork. The garden fork has wide blades that are thin and sharp. The pitch fork has round tines that are very pointed at the end.

The garden fork is designed so that it can be forced into the ground like a digging shovel or spade. But you need an extra rocking action to break the load of dirt free. If you are working very hard ground, you may even bend or break the tines. If you use a garden fork with a short handle, you can aggravate any back problems.

A long-handled spading fork is the best tool to use in light soils. You must keep the cutting edges of any fork sharp, however. An ordinary file will sharpen the fork's blades.

The lifting fork, usually called the pitch fork, is designed for use with hay and straw. The sharp points force the tool into the hay and straw, and catch it on tightly. The implement is designed with a long handle to afford good swinging power to carry the load over a distance. If you try digging into the earth with a lifting fork you will bend the tines and probably not get much earth out anyway.

Garden trowel. The garden trowel is simply a miniature spade for use in turning loose soil near a plant. The tool can be easily bent or twisted if it is used in anything but the very softest earth or sand. Most of the garden trowels available are made of pressed metal and will bend or crack under any kind of strain or pressure.

A trowel made of forged metal gives much better service. Use a trowel with a blade that is not excessively long, or you will chance breaking or bending it. Do not bother getting a trowel with an extra long handle; it is often a liability rather than an asset. Always keep the blade of any trowel sharp. Filing will do the trick.

Generally speaking, the spade, fork and trowel are the three main hand digging

Spading fork (left) has wide, sharp blades for digging into the earth and turning quantities of soil. A spading fork usually has four blades, rarely more. Pitch fork (center) is designed with thin, round blades shaped to stick into bunches of hay or piles of grass and leaves to lift and carry them. Note that pitch fork has six blades. Garden trowel (right) is used for light work in soil around flowers and plants. It becomes useless if the blade is bent. Trowel made of forged metal will give the best service.

tools you need for garden work. The main digging power tool is the rotary tiller, which performs the operations of all three hand tools in a faster, more efficient way.

Rotary tiller. A power tiller can turn heavily compacted soil in aerated, pulverized, well-textured planting turf within minutes. During the tilling operation, the rotary tiller works fertilizer and soil amendments like compost into the soil thoroughly, far more completely than you can with hand tools.

A rotary tiller can do all these things for you:

Aerate the soil

Prepare a plant bed

Remove dead plants and weeds

Plant rows weed-free

Mix in organic materials

Blend plant foods together

Mulch

The power tiller comes in many sizes, from a small electric model, usually called a cultivator, to one the size of a walking tractor. The small tiller works to a maximum depth of 5 or 6 inches. The tiller with a gasoline engine will work down to 12 to 28 inches. In between there are three or four different-sized gas-operated models:

(1) Lightweight. 3 to 3½ horsepower engine. Tills to a depth of 5 to 6 inches, 12 to 24 inches wide.

(2) Medium size. 4 HP. 7 to 8″ deep, 12 to 26″ wide.

(3) Heavyweight. 5 HP. 6 to 10″ deep, 12 to 28″ wide.

(4) Professional. 5–8 HP. 14″ deep, 40″ wide.

If you do not wish to buy a tiller, you can always rent one for use during any season you need it. Or you can team up with a neighbor and each pay a part of the cost of a medium-sized machine. It is probably best to rent one before you decide to buy. Using it will give you a good idea of what size you want.

Deere & Company

Walk-behind power rotary tiller can be used to thoroughly mulch and cultivate a garden.

Here are some points to look for in a rotary tiller:

(1) Speeds. You should have one or more forward speeds, neutral, and reverse. You should have efficient, fast-acting controls to keep the machine from getting out of hand.

(2) Solid construction. The deeper you plan to dig, the stronger the unit. Tilling 2 to 3 inches for a flower bed is quite a different proposition from tilling to a depth of 6 to 10 inches to mix in fertilizer.

(3) Engine. The engine should deliver from 3 to 5 horsepower; it should be well-shielded from dust and dirt.

(4) Good balance. If the balance is good, you will get better tillage. A few pounds of pressure will lift the tines; you can turn better, too.

(5) Proper weight disbursement. The engine should be mounted directly over the tines to give the best lugging power.

(6) Tines. Three kinds of tines are usually available: slasher, bolo, and pick. Slasher tines are used for cultivating, tilling and mulching heavy soil. Bolo tines are used for thorough tilling and cultivating in most soils, but especially for cutting up weeds and weed roots. Pick tines are used to deal with hard, heavy problem soil.

(7) Adjustable depth control. You should be able to adjust the tines to control tilling depth.

(8) Remote controls. You should be able to reach the operating controls on the handle without extra effort.

(9) Gear housing. The gears take most of the wear and tear on a tiller. A worm-and-gear drive that runs in oil or a roller-chain-and-sprocket drive that runs in oil both come on quality units.

(10) Attachments. The following attachments are available, although not on any one machine: extension tines; furrower; hiller; lawn edger; aerator; snow and dozer blades; sickle mower; cultivator; weed knives; lawn roller; plow; harrow; leveling drag; cultivating shield; transport wheels; fenders; ditcher; tractor tires; and mold-board plows.

Be sure to get a one-year warranty on the entire unit—not just on the engine.

LOADING TOOLS. The shovel and fork have already been explained in detail in the preceding discussion on hand tools used for digging.

TRANSPORTING TOOLS. For carrying work, the most important machine in the gardener's arsenal is the wheelbarrow or the garden cart. You will need one or the other for any general garden work you do. Either one will carry soil, debris, sand, branches, cuttings, grass clippings, and so on.

The wheelbarrow has only one wheel, and the garden cart two. The fact that the brunt of the load rests on the two wheels in the middle of the garden cart gives it a slight advantage over the wheelbarrow where the load rests on the arms of the operator.

Whatever you buy, get a good strong carrier. Do not stint on price. And do not buy one that won't carry at least 3 to 4 cubic feet of material. Be sure to get one that has either inflatable or semi-pneumatic tires.

SPREADING TOOLS. Every garden needs some kind of spreading mechanism not only for broadcasting grass seed but also for disseminating plant food and fertilizer. The average spreader is a wheeled unit carrying a container with controlled dissemination holes that can be regulated for an exact flow of material. As the operator

1TD

Ordinary garden wheelbarrow is designed to carry soil, debris, sand, branches, cuttings, grass clippings — in short, almost anything you want to tote from one place to another.

MTD

Garden cart has two wheels instead of wheelbarrow's one, and should be built to carry at least 3 to 4 cubic feet of load.

pushes the unit across the ground, the action of the wheels forces the material through the broadcast holes. The holes can be opened and shut by a hand lever which the operator manipulates as he walks along.

A spreader that seeds or fertilizes a 20- to 24-inch wide pattern is usually big enough for the average suburban lot. A 24-inch wide spreader holds about 75 pounds of dry fertilizer.

There are some spreaders that spray both seed and fertilizer out away from the container as the operator pushes it along.

There are even several power spreaders available; you sit in a tractor-like seat and ride along behind the seeder or fertilizer. These are usually used on acreage larger than the suburban lot.

Allis-Chalmers Corp.

Handy power dump cart is used for hauling wood, rock, dirt, and other heavy items around yard. It is made to hook up to a riding mower or garden tractor.

CUTTING TOOLS. Cutting tools for garden use can be divided into two distinct types: those for cutting grass; and those for cutting and pruning shrubs, hedges, and trees.

Tools used for cutting and trimming grass are covered in detail in Chapter 3, Grass Maintenance. This discussion is concerned only with cutting tools used in shrub, hedge, and tree work. Such tools are called pruning tools.

Garden pruning tools include several different types for different work: shears, saw, and knife.

Shears. Garden shears come in two models: one whose blades pass each other like a pair of common household scissors; and one whose cutting blade presses directly against an anvil blade. You can use either type for work around the garden. Each gives a clean cut, essential for all pruning work.

Assortment of garden cutting tools include the following: *A—D*, hedge shears; *E, F, G*, lopping shears; *H—K*, grass shears; *L, M*, sickles; *N, O, P*, pruning shears; and *Q, R*, grass whips.

Disston Corp.

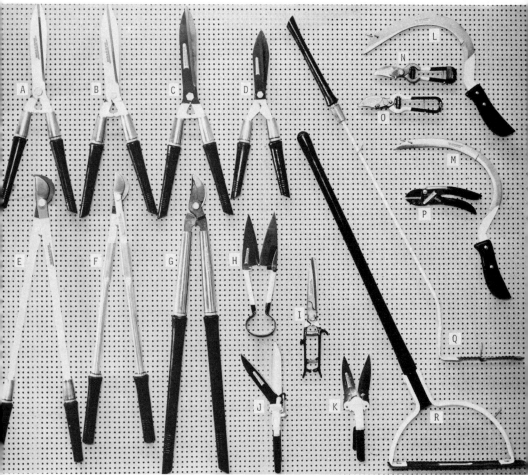

Ames Corp.

Grass shears are designed for cutting unmowed turf near edgings, brick walks, pavement, curbs, and borders or obstructions of any kind around a lawn. This model is activated by vertical hand pressure.

Deere & Company

Power grass shears are operated by a rechargeable battery inside a hand-held machine. Pressure activates blade and lock switch keeps blade running until switched off.

Hardware and Industrial Products

Hedge shears will shape and prune all types of flowering shrubs, needle-leaved and broad-leaved evergreens, as well as other types of plants set out to form hedges.

There are five sizes of shears, each used for slightly different shearing tasks:
(1) Grass shears.
(2) Flower shears.
(3) Pruning shears.
(4) Hedge shears.
(5) Lopping shears.

Grass shears come in many different models: scissor type; single-action type: floating blade type; horizontal action type. Most grass shears measure from 10 to 13 inches in length; a pair can be used interchangeably for work with smaller shrubs and hedges.

Flower shears are designed to cut and hold thorny or hard-to-reach flowers so you can remove the flower in the grip of the shears. Flower shears measure about 6 inches long.

Pruning shears are designed to cut branches up to about ³/₄ inch thick. Designed usually with an anvil type action, they are used for shrubs, bushes, ornamentals, vines, and so on. Many varieties are available, usually from 7 to 8 inches in length.

Hedge shears are designed for special work with hedges and shrubs. Many of these can be used not only for hedges and shrubs but for grass trimming as well. Some have single serrated blades to grip the branch and hold it while the cutting blade works against it. Most hedge shears run from 16 inches to 24 inches in length.

Lopping shears are designed for heavy cutting work in hedges, shrubs, and trees. A lopping shear usually has a hook and blade combined for cutting. It can take branches up to 1¹/₄-inch in diameter. The average is about 30 inches in length, although some are as short as 21 inches.

Power shears. The hedge trimmer is simply a power tool that simultaneously operates several dozen miniature shears over an extended portion of a shrub or hedge. Its design resembles two double-edged rakes working against each other. Each tooth becomes a cutter working against a counter-tooth on the other blade. One blade is stationary; the other moves up and down continuously.

The hedge trimmer can be powered either by electricity from a power outlet, or by a rechargeable battery in the tool itself. The only problem with operating from a power outlet is that the trimmer cannot be used any farther than the end of the cord. Also there is the imminent possibility that the operator may accidentally cut the cord in two.

The problem with the battery-operated hedge trimmer is that the battery must be recharged before each use. The average battery-operated hedge trimmer will usually

Pruning shears are used for all types of cutting, shaping, and trimming of general overhead or ground-level flowering shrubs, evergreens, trees, roses, and broad-leaved evergreens like laurel and rhododendron.

Lopping shears are used for pruning low limbs of trees and ornamental shrubs, and for shaping larger evergreens. When branches of woody specimens like laurel and rhododendron are thick, lopping shears are better to use than pruning shears.

Seymour Smith & Son, Inc.   *Seymour Smith & Son, Inc.*

Hardware and Industrial Products

Pruning saw is used for heavy work on large limbs and tough branches. Full length of blade is 24 inches; it may be curved for working in close quarters.

finish a good-sized hedge before it runs out. Most rechargeable batteries can be recharged five hundred times.

There are various sizes of hedge trimmers, each designed for different performance and usage. Lightness, toughness, and durability are prime requisites for any one of them.

You can use a smaller model, say one with a 16-inch cut, operated by a $^1/_{10}$ horsepower motor, with a weight of about 5$^3/_4$ pounds; or you can use a 30-inch model driven by a $^1/_5$ horsepower motor, with a weight of 8 pounds. With the latter, you can shape the top and sides of a 100-foot hedge in about fifteen minutes.

Saws. Pruning saws come in two models for use in the garden as cutting instruments: one resembles an ordinary carpenter's saw; and the other resembles a hack saw with a steel bow-back. Both types are for use as heavy-duty cutting tools in tree pruning work.

The pruning saw is similar to a carpenter's saw, except that many are shaped in curves to facilitate work in cramped positions in trees. Some have straight blades. They run from 14 inches to 24 inches in length.

The bow saw is designed with a metal frame to keep tension on the blade clamped between its ends. The bow saw is usually around 2 feet long, with some as short as 21 inches and some as long as 30 inches.

Power saws. The chain saw is certainly worth considering if you have a fireplace and burn your own wood in it. It is also a desirable tool to have if you are stuck with a lot of large branches to remove from timber.

Chain saws are powered by gasoline or by electricity.

The electric chain saw is usually used for lighter work with wood up to 1 foot in diameter. The best size electric for the average homeowner is a 1 horsepower saw weighing from 8 to 12 pounds.

The gasoline chain saw is widely available, usually powered by a 2-cycle gas engine. The chain saw is rated in cubic-inch displacement of the engine; a unit of 4.7 cubic inches or less will service the average home owner. Models come in many lengths. An 18-inch bar can cut through a 1$^1/_2$ foot hardwood log in 24 seconds.

Check out the weight of the chain saw you buy, however, before you put your money down. If it is too heavy, it can really tire you out. Buy a model with enough power and just barely long enough a bar for your needs — but no more.

You can use a chain saw for felling small trees that get in the way of your bigger growth, for cutting brush and saplings, and for pruning certain large growths. You can use a chain saw for rough carpentry, too.

Disston Corp.

Hardware and Industrial Products

Bow saw is designed to cut branches of trees. Bow keeps blade springy even though it is made thin in order to avoid binding when cutting green wood.

Safety-lock folding saw is ideal portable tool for medium-sized branches. It weighs about 9 ounces, and locks in open and closed positions. Tool can be used where bow saw and pruning saw can't reach.

Extra-long tree pruner will telescope out from 6 feet to 12, providing cutting action on branches up to 1¼ inches in diameter.

Most chain saws, like this one, will cut logs, firewood, and fence posts, and will trim tree limbs, clear brush, and small trees.

Seymour Smith & Son, Inc.

Allis-Chalmers Corp

Rent a chain saw first and try it out to see if you really need it. By using it you can get an idea of its performance and what it can and cannot do. If you simply want to cut down two or three trees, rent a saw; there is no need to buy one for a simple one-time-a-year job like that.

Knives. Certain lopping shears are designed so that they are actually knives rather than shears. A lopping shears with an extension handle is designed for use on tall trees. The knife is operated against an anvil by means of a rope or pulley, the pruner holds the knife against the branch to be cut, and manipulated the knife from below.

CHOPPING TOOLS. The hoe and the cultivator are the standard garden tools for chopping out weeds, unneeded plants, and anything else that is in the way of proper cultivation of the soil. There are two kinds of hoe used by the suburban gardener: the garden hoe; and the scuffle hoe.

Garden hoe. The garden hoe has a flat bottom, and a blade that is set at just about right angles to the handle. A blade 4 by 6 inches is a good size to use. The garden hoe is used for chopping out weeds, particularly in hard earth. It is used to pile earth up around the base of a plant—called "earthing up." And it can serve to raise hills on which seeds are sown.

Scuffle hoe. The scuffle hoe has a pointed blade. It is used for working in rows of vegetables and rows of garden flowers. The pointed end cuts out weeds and loosens surface soil. It can also be used for digging a straight ditch to plant seeds in a row.

Cultivator. The third implement for chopping is the pronged cultivator. This is a 3- or 4-tined tool that looks like a pitchfork with the teeth bent like claws. It is smaller than a fork, of course, and is used for eradicating weeds, especially in terrain full of stones. It can also pull out unwanted plants.

Garden hoe, designed with flat bottom, is used as shown to move dirt around near plants. It can also be used to shop up dry soil and loosen it for working.

Deere ½ Company

Scuffle hoe has a sharp point for digging small indented rows for seeding, irrigation, or fertilizing the soil.

W. R. Grace & Co.

Hand cultivator can be used for small garden jobs like planting flowers or shrubs, or for preparing a section in a lawn for reseeding.

True Temper Corp.

Cultivator with pitchfork-type blades is used for larger cultivating jobs, like preparing garden row for planting, or scratching below surface of dirt to loosen hard clods.

Two models are available: one with a 4-foot handle for stand-up work; the other with a 12- to 18-inch handle for close to the earth work.

These chopping tools can all be used for aeration and for tilling and cultivation of all kinds.

Power chopper. One of the most difficult jobs around the homesite is getting rid of leaves and branches that fall from the trees. Of course you can rake them up, but then you have the job of piling them in a compost heap and waiting for them to rot.

There are power machines that do that job better than nature or the home gardener. A power shredder can reduce a yardful of leaves, weeds, or vegetable matter in minutes to shredded material rich enough for the compost heap.

You can use the material for mulching, too, exactly as you would use peat moss, buckwheat hulls, or any other commercially available material. Or you can put it in the compost heap for next season.

The shredder can also be used for mixing soil, peat, and various organic wastes, lime and fertilizer together into potting or bedding soil for special garden beds.

The material treated by a power shredder is uniformly shredded and in excellent condition for decomposition.

There are big shredders that take branches up to $3\frac{1}{2}$ inches thick — but these are actually mulching machines. However, you can always rent one if you have a lot of branches to chew up.

Combination garden hoe-rake can be quickly turned over after hoeing to rake dirt. Combination is used both in garden and lawn projects.

Newly designed cultivator is used for weeding in close areas around fences, shrubs, and buildings. It can be used for mulching and reseeding, without removing topsoil.

Ames Corp.

The average sized shredder takes branches up to about 1 inch thick, but is mostly concerned with chewing leaves down to size.

A shredder is composed of a funnel that directs the leaves and branches down into the cutting section where whirling cutters spin between stationary cutters, chewing the material and blowing it out into a bag attached to the outlet vent.

RAKING TOOLS. The two types of rakes used in the garden—iron and bamboo or spring-steel—are used for separate operations.

The iron rake, which is square-shaped and made of tough metal, is used to rake over the soil just before sowing seeds. It is also used for raking up debris from the lawn.

196

Power-operated mulcher-shredder-bagger can cut up yard debris and reduce the volume more than 80 percent, forcing it into large, detachable plastic bag.

Toro Mfg. Corp.

The bamboo rake, which is fan-shaped, is used to remove leaves and grass clippings from the lawn. Like the metal rake made of spring steel, which it resembles, it will not tear out grass, but springs away, taking leaves and debris with it and leaving the grass unhurt.

Power rake. To break up thatch—accumulated grass cuttings on the surface of the soil—in a more efficient manner than an operator can with a hand rake, a power dethatcher is available, run by gasoline.

The dethatcher-aerator consists of a revolving drum mounted with rows of closely spaced spring-mounted tines (like a series of metal rakes). As the machine rolls along, the drum revolves over the ground, brushing the tines across the surface of the soil, whipping the thatch loose. The thatch can then be removed by the use of a enabling you to mow up to the edge without any hindrance.

The tines break up the surface of the soil, helping aerate the turf. With the soil aired, it is easier to seed and fertilize.

When you use a dethatcher-aerator, be sure to experiment and get the setting of the tines exactly right. Tines cutting too deeply into the soil will tear up turf; if they do not cut deeply enough, they will leave the thatch untouched.

Power sweeper. Getting material up off the lawn is a tough job by hand, but a sweeper, vacuum, or blower can do the job in minutes. These are all machines powered by gasoline that can be pushed by hand or can even be pulled behind a garden tractor (see below).

When leaves are dry, the sweeper will do a fine job of picking up for you. It can pick up grass clippings after each cutting. A rotary brush lifts the leaves and clippings right out of the lawn and throws them back into a large hopper for collection.

Atwater Strong Co. Inc.

Power blower tidies up grass cuttings, leaves, and yard debris by pushing them into compact heap in one corner of yard.

The yard vacuum works exactly like an indoor vacuum does. It sucks up leaves and cuttings and collects them in an enormous bag attached to the unit as you push it along over the ground.

The blower, or air broom, works in an opposite fashion from the vacuum. It *blows* leaves into a pile, as the operator circles around the yard from the outside perimeter to the center. Once the pile is established, the material can be bagged and taken away.

Both the air broom and the yard vacuum have a hose attachment that you can use to reach in and around shrubs and foundation plants to blow out or pick up leaves and trash that accumulates there.

Sweeper, vacuum and blower are useful all through the outdoor living season. They work on driveways, walks, and terraces. The leaf and grass material can be compacted into about $1/10$ of its original size, giving you good prospects for speedy removal of all debris.

PRYING TOOLS. In some situations where there are a great number of rocks and stones in the ground, you will find a spade and/or shovel is not enough to dig a good hole for a plant or tree.

It is always good to have a wrecking bar around the house just in case. This bar, made of heavy steel, and running about 3 to 4 feet in length, can be used to jam down between two rocks wedged in the ground to pry them apart. Once the rocks are twisted loose from the impacted soil, it is a much simpler matter to pull them out by hand.

ALL-PURPOSE TOOL. The garden tractor is one of the most versatile power tools the suburban homeowner has at his command. Attachments are available that will permit the tractor to do each one of the nine gardening actions already discussed.

Crowbar or prybar is a valuable tool for garden work, especially in loosening and moving rock or other tightly wedged objects. The bar also helps in digging with a spade through tightly impacted gravel.

Therefore, the tractor deserves a special section all by itself.

As with a rotary tiller, you may not want to buy a tractor for yourself; you may want to share the cost with a neighbor; or you may want to rent one for a day or two when you need it. A tractor is a powerful machine, and can be dangerous if improperly handled. You should practice with one until you know you can master it before you go ahead to use it. Don't even climb into the seat of one until you read the instruction manual thoroughly.

If you have a big enough yard, and if you want fast, efficient, all-around service, the garden tractor is your baby: gasoline-powered or battery-powered.

For a start, here's what it will do:

Plow	Reap	Dethatch
Till	Roll a lawn	Aerate
Grade	Bulldoze	Generate electric power
Rake	Spread seed	Pull a garden cart
Mow	Fertilize	

Models and types. A great variety of farm and garden tractors are available. Because garden tractors are used for shorter hauls and because they do not need to be as rugged as heavy-duty farm tractors, they have been refined into more easily-operated vehicles.

Some gasoline-operated garden tractors run almost exactly like an automatic-transmission automobile, with similar gear and steering-wheel action. Most have hydrostatic transmissions controlled by a foot pedal or a hand lever, so that there is no need to shift gears. These machines range in power from 12 to 18 horsepower.

In addition to gasoline-powered tractors, there are electric garden tractors, also ranging from 12 to 18 horsepower. The electric tractor uses a rechargeable battery that can be recharged in five hours on house current. The tractor is operated by means of a lever: forward moves the tractor ahead with speed control determined by the position of the lever; backward the same.

Horsepower. As you can see by scanning the list of jobs the average garden tractor can perform, many of them duplicate work done by attachments available for a walking rotary tiller.

In fact, most of these jobs can also be performed by attachments fitted to a riding

Garden tractor can be a versatile suburban yard aid. Most models are gas-operated and run like an ordinary car. Tractor can do a large number of garden jobs with attachments like this lawn roller.

General Electric Corp.

FMC Bolens Cor

Electric garden tractor performs pretty much like the gas-operated model. This photo shows the action of tiller attachment used for mulching and cultivating.

Allis-Chalmers Corp.

Moldboard plow is a special attachment for a garden tractor. Like the moldboard on a bulldozer, the plow turns the soil and thrusts it to one side as the tractor passes.

Tiller attachment on the rear of garden tractor tills soil with a wide sweep, pulverizing and mixing it.

Deere & Company

Power sprayer can be attached to any garden tractor for quick, accurate operation.

Deere & Company

Deere & Company

Power sweeper attachment on garden tractor sucks up cuttings, leaves, and debris of all kinds. Full bag can then be detached and removed.

Ariens Company

Snow blade behind garden tractor is capable of seven different positions for snow-removal chores. Blade can be positioned straight ahead or rotated left or right 25 degrees.

Sickle-bar mower can be lowered to right of garden tractor for reaping or mowing grass or weeds.

Deere & Company

Snow thrower attachment, mounted on garden tractor, casts snow out through an adjustable vent.

Murray Ohio Mfg. Co.

Power broom attachment is a versatile performer, removing thatch from lawns and sweeping up cuttings in summer and brooming off light snowfalls in winter.

Ariens Company

mower, discussed in Chapter 3. In spite of the confusion and overlap, there are fairly clear-cut distinctions between riding mowers, walking tillers, and garden tractors:

(1) Most walking rotary tillers range from 3 to 8 horsepower, with the smallest especially designed for the average garden. (See beginning of this chapter.)

(2) Most riding mowers specifically designed to cut grass deliver from about 4 to 6 horsepower. Larger machines—from 7 to 15 horsepower—are actually tractors that are designed to do many jobs.

(3) In the 6- to 8-horsepower range there is a great deal of overlapping between riding mowers and garden tractors.

(4) Garden tractors in the range from 12 to 18 horsepower can generally perform most all the actions of a farm tractor, including light bulldozing—particularly for snow removal.

Four objectives. In shopping for a garden tractor, be sure the machine fulfills these four required objectives:

(1) It is small enough for you to operate without difficulty.

(2) It is large enough and powerful enough to do all the jobs you want it to do.

(3) It can effectively handle each job you want it to do.

(4) It is safe and convenient to operate.

Check list. Below is a check list of features that you should look for in an ideal tractor. No single tractor has all these features, but each will have some.

(1) At least 6 horsepower in a brand-name engine.

(2) No more than 12 horsepower.

(3) A minimum of three speeds forward, and one in reverse.

(4) Big wheels with wide tires or heavy-ribbed tires if you expect to draw a heavy load.

(5) Easy-steering front wheels with enough tire to avoid digging into the lawn.

(6) A chassis heavy enough to connect front end to back.

(7) A locking differential for maximum traction.

(8) Power take-off available at the side (front and back).

(9) An instrument panel of the automobile type.

(10) A steering wheel adjustable to different heights.

(11) A lever to raise and lower attachments.

(12) A clutch and brake on one pedal.

(14) Clearance of from 7 to 9 inches under the machine.

(14) A hood that covers and protects, but opens easily.

(15) A gas tank you can fill without lifting the hood. (Not applicable to a battery-powered machine.)

Tractor attachments. You'll find a list of accessories available for the tractor in which you're interested. Study the list and get the ones you need. Instruction manuals will tell you exactly how to use each attachment. Be sure you practice safety methods when you use any of the accessories.

Here is a check list of features that you should be able to get for a tractor:

Grader	Rotary tiller	Three-gang mower
Bulldozer blade	Spreader	2400-watt generator
Snow-blower	Rotary mower	Planter-fertilizer
Sickle bar for tall growth	Roller	Sweeper
Plow	Dump cart	Rotary rake
Disk harrow	Two-wheel cart	Air compressor
Hydraulic lift	Spiker-aerator	Big-capacity water pump
		Side-mounting cordwood saw

Index